THEOLOGICAL
HIGHLIGHTS
OF
VATICAN II

THEOLOGICAL HIGHLIGHTS OF VATICAN II

Joseph Ratzinger

now Pope Benedict XVI
with an Introduction by Thomas P. Rausch, SJ

Paulist Press
New York/Mahwah, NJ

First published by Paulist Press, 1966, by special arrangement with Verlag J. P. Bachem in Köln. The German editions were translated by Henry Traub, SJ (Part I), Gerard C. Thormann, PhD (Parts II and III), Werner Barzel (Part IV).

NIHIL OBSTAT:
Rev. James J. O'Connor
Censor Librorum

IMPRIMATUR:
+ Leo A. Pursley, DD
Bishop of Fort Wayne–South Bend

October 24, 1966

Library of Congress Cataloging-in-Publication Data
Benedict XVI, Pope, 1927–
    Theological highlights of Vatican II / Joseph Ratzinger (now Pope Benedict XVI) ; with an Introduction by Thomas P. Rausch. — [Rev. ed.].
        p. cm.
    Includes bibliographical references.
    ISBN 978-0-8091-4610-9 (alk. paper)
    1. Vatican Council (2nd : 1962–1965) I. Title.
    BX830.1962.B46 2009
    262´.52—dc22

                                                    2009023555

Cover Design by Lynn Else

Published by Paulist Press
997 Macarthur Boulevard
Mahwah, NJ 07430

www.paulistpress.com

Printed and bound in the
United States of America

CONTENTS

Preface to the English Edition vii

Introduction by Thomas P. Rausch, SJ 1

PART ONE: THE FIRST SESSION
   I. Opening of the Council and Election
      of the Commissions 19
  II. First Debates on the Liturgy Schema.................28
 III. Early Debate on Revelation...............................40
 IV. Last Phase of the First Session 49

PART TWO: THE SECOND SESSION
   I. Preliminary Notes..57
  II. Work Begins: The Debate on the Church..........71
 III. Practical Questions: Bishops' Conferences,
      Bishops' Council and Curial Reform 91
 IV. Interlude: The Mariological Question 94
  V. The Question of Ecumenism 96
 VI. The Achievements of the Second Session........118
VII. Afterword...122

PART THREE: THE THIRD SESSION

   I.   The Fall of 1964.................................127
  II. The Council at the Close of the Session..........151
 III. Ecumenical Problems Involved in the
       Teaching on Episcopal Collegiality.................161
 IV. Concluding Remarks 192

PART FOUR: THE FOURTH SESSION

   I.   Opening of the Session and the
       New Synod of Bishops 199
  II. The First Topic of Debate: Religious Liberty ...206
 III. The Struggle over Schema 13 212
 IV. The Council's Two Final Discussions..............244
  V. The Last Phase of the Council 253
 VI. Epilogue..259

CONTENTS

PREFACE TO THE ENGLISH EDITION

This book was originally published in four separate booklets which appeared after each of the four sessions of Vatican Council II. In each I tried to give an account of what had happened during that particular session and a preview of what still remained to be done. The four parts of the present book correspond to the four original booklets.

Thus this book clearly has its own specific character. It is not an attempt to appraise past events from the detached viewpoint of the historian. Rather, it is the account of a personal journey through the landscape of each session, with an open view toward future developments. Therefore, the various parts invite the reader to reacquaint himself with the Council, moving through it again from its beginnings. He is invited to reexperience the step-by-step movement from present to future rather than merely contemplate the end result from afar. This is no make-believe journey. The Council, as an event in the Church, is still a matter of unfinished business. It must be grasped this way. It is not a collection of clear-cut recipes.

The Council's statements are not a body of purely intellectual teaching; still less are they simply a collection of technical and pragmatic directives. They are the product of a spiritual process. A process or movement can only be comprehended by participating in it, by gradual, step-by-step, obedient involvement in it. We would misunderstand the Council's teaching were we to take it as a sudden switchover, a sudden shift from "conservatism" to "progressivism" in the Church. Ultimately the Council sought simply to do at the present time what the Church's proclamation is supposed to do at all times: to lead the way on the journey of faith. This journey began with God's call to Abraham to leave the land of his fathers and to set out toward the land of promise.

Thus the intention of this modest book should be sufficiently clear. It does not contain a chronicle of external happenings or a description of the factors at work behind the scenes; other writers have already reported on this at great length. Rather, this is an attempt to delineate the inner aspects, the spiritual profile of the Council. Thus it aims to point up the perspective of Council events which is more important than diplomatic factors, intramural power plays and antagonism among groups—the kind of thing that has so greatly stirred public attention during recent years. For such a study as this, the use (all too prevalent today) of clichés such as "conservative" and "progressive" seems inadequate. The renewal of the Church, in which the author in his capacity as Council *peritus* has in his own way collaborated, cannot mean progress in the sense of technological and economic development. This renewal has rather a twofold intention. Its point of reference is contemporary man in his reality and in his world, taken as it is. But the measure of the renewal is Christ, as scripture witnesses him. And if the renewal seeks to think through and to speak the Gospel of Christ in a way understandable to contemporary man— i.e., in a contemporary fashion (*aggiornamento* means bringing up to date), then the objective is precisely that Christ may become understood. The consequence of this is that the person to whom Christ has been taken can now begin to betake himself to Christ—he who encompasses our yesterday and our tomorrow in the today of his everlasting life. It is such an *aggiornamento* that this book seeks to serve—an updating aimed at finding a pathway from our transitory today into the never-ending today of the Lord.

—Tübingen, September 2, 1966

PREFACE TO THE ENGLISH EDITION

INTRODUCTION

When the Second Vatican Council opened in October of 1962, among the *periti* or scholarly experts brought to Rome by the bishops was a young professor from Bonn, Joseph Ratzinger. Though only thirty-five years old, Ratzinger was already a rising star. His courses on Catholic fundamental theology were popular, based more on the fathers of the Church than on the neo-scholasticism then dominant. His courses also included lectures on Protestant works, unusual for a Catholic theologian in those days. While at Bonn, Hubert Luthe, a former classmate and later bishop of Essen, introduced him to Cardinal Joseph Frings, the archbishop of Cologne. Impressed with the young professor, Frings brought Ratzinger to Rome for the Council as his theological advisor, where he was to help shape some of its most significant documents.

Joseph Ratzinger was born in 1927 in Marktl am Inn on the Austrian border, the youngest of three children in a deeply Catholic Bavarian family. His father was a rural policeman, known for his anti-Nazi views.

Ratzinger's studies for the priesthood, begun at the minor seminary at Traunstein in 1939, were interrupted by the war. His seminary class was assigned to an antiaircraft "Flak" battery in 1943, and a year later he was drafted into a labor battalion. He never saw combat. After Hitler's suicide he left for home, trying to avoid the SS who were executing those they suspected of deserting in the final days of the war. Captured by American troops at his home, he was sent to a prisoner of war camp outside Ulm for a few weeks, resuming his studies in the fall, first at Freising, then in 1947 at the Herzogliches Georgianum, a theological institute affiliated with the University of Munich. He was ordained at Freising together with his brother Georg on June 29, 1951, and completed his doctorate at Munich a year later.

In 1959 he was appointed to the chair in fundamental theology at Bonn. From Bonn, Ratzinger moved to academic positions at Münster (1963), Tübingen (1966), and Regensburg (1969). In 1976 he was named archbishop of Munich and Freising. Pope Paul VI named him to the college of cardinals in June 1977, and in 1981 Pope John Paul II appointed him prefect of the Congregation for the Doctrine of the Faith. After John Paul II's death, Ratzinger was elected bishop of Rome on April 19, 2005, taking the name Benedict XVI.

Report on the Council

The English version of Ratzinger's *Theological Highlights of Vatican II* was originally published in Germany as four separate booklets, one appearing after each of the four sessions of the Council (1962–65). The book captures some of the drama of the Council, as well as its emotional climate: the problems of how to work effectively with 2,900 fathers—including bishops, auxiliary bishops, abbots, and superiors of orders—although the actual number attending decreased to about 2,000; the overwhelming number of schemata, some seventy, facing the fathers at the beginning of the Council; the fact that few of the bishops had any parliamentary or synodal experience; the fatigue after the difficult first session; the uncertainty about the Council's future after the death of Pope John XXIII; the revived optimism at the beginning of the fourth session after the general secretary read the pope's *motu proprio* establishing the Synod of Bishops; and the tumultuous applause that greeted the symbolic kiss of peace between Pope Paul and the representative of Patriarch Athenagoras at the end of the Council.

Both a report on the debates and struggles that made up each session, as well as a theological commentary, the book shows Ratzinger on the side of the Council's progressive wing. He saw the problem of papal centralism as evident to all, and as an obstacle to Christian unity. Frequently underlining the need for reform of the Roman curia, he noted that, aside from the pope, it seemed to be "the only really formative and active authority in the Church" and that tensions between the bishops and the curia were not something recent, but went back as far as the late Middle Ages. The Council had begun to change the situation; the bishops were starting to discover themselves as an episcopate, with their own powers and collective responsibility, and their episcopal conferences as a quasi-synodal agency between the individual bishops and the pope. Ratzinger welcomed the establishment of the Synod of Bishops, seeing it as a promising renewal of the structure of the Church. At the same time, from the beginning of the book he rejects the popular view that the Council marked a "switch" from conservatism to progressivism in the Church. His own views, with a couple of exceptions, have remained remarkably consistent over the years.

Ratzinger does acknowledge elsewhere that his views on the liturgical movement have changed. At the time of the Council he was hopeful about liturgical reform. He lamented after the first session that the 2,500 bishops and faithful present at the opening liturgy were reduced to mere spectators, called for more active participation of the laity, and applauded the decentralization of liturgical decision making, allowing the various conferences of bishops to formulate, within limits, their own liturgical laws. Quoting St. Paul on the importance of intelligible language, he argued against the untouchability of Latin, saying that as a liturgical language it was dead and needed to give way. The example of the Eastern Churches offered a helpful corrective to Latin exclusivity. Several times he referred to the "archaizing" of the liturgy, which since Trent had become "a rigid, fixed and firmly encrusted system," making the acute observation that none of the saints of the Catholic Reformation drew their spirituality from the liturgy. In *Milestones*, a personal memoir first published in 1997, he acknowledges that he saw the principles of the liturgical movement as a marvelous point of departure for the Council, but continues, "I was not able to foresee that the negative sides of the liturgical movement would afterward reemerge with redoubled strength, almost to the point of pushing the liturgy towards its own self-destruction."[1]

As a *peritus* Ratzinger worked on the Dogmatic Constitution on Divine Revelation (*Dei Verbum*), the Dogmatic Constitution on the Church (*Lumen gentium*), the Pastoral Constitution on the Church in the Modern World (*Gaudium et spes*),[2] and the Decree on the Missionary Activity of the Church (*Ad gentes*). Topics he treats in detail in the book include the debate on the liturgy schema, the early debate on divine revelation, the questions of Mariology and ecumenism, the decree on the bishops' office in the Church, religious liberty, the Church and the Jews, and the schemas on the missions and on priestly ministry and life. He gives special attention to the Dogmatic Constitution on the Church and to the Pastoral Constitution on the Church in the Modern World.

The Debate on the Church

Ratzinger's discussion of the Council's second session explores at some length the procedural problems faced by the Council fathers. These began to change with the election of Cardinal Montini as Pope Paul VI. Calling for a reform of the curia, the pope subsequently took a number of important steps. He revised the Council's statutes to improve its workings; created a new governing body, which consisted of four moderators, who were generally more progressive cardinals; strengthened the conciliar commissions by expanding their membership, with new members chosen partly by election by the council fathers and partly by papal appointment; allowed for the first time members of the Council to submit items for discussion, rather than reserving this privilege to the pope; and made it possible for laypeople to participate as auditors, including some women. They could be consulted by the commissions or could even address the plenary assembly.

The first draft of the constitution on the Church was rejected. Ratzinger describes the new text, drafted by a group of theologians associated with Cardinal Suenens, as a "leap forward." It complemented the idea of the Church as the Body of Christ with that of the People of God and described the Church as determined by pneumatological as well as christological elements, being both charismatic and sacramental in its structure. Other significant aspects include the idea of the Church as "the Church of the poor," advocated by bishops from Latin countries. Ratzinger comments sympathetically that the Church "has for a long time looked like a Church of baroque princes." Also important was the emphasis on the Church as sacrament.

The most controversial subject was episcopal collegiality, taking up more time than any other issue. It was opposed not just by many representatives of the curia, but also by the majority of the ecumenical observers, at least until the beginning of the third session, for it also involved the question of the Church and the churches. Though he does not mention this, Ratzinger played a key role in shaping article 22 of *Lumen gentium* on the nature of collegiality; he drew up an important report arguing that one became a member of the episcopal college "in virtue of his consecration and his communion with the head."[3] He refers to this as an "inconspicuous little statement." But besides emphasizing the importance of communion with the bishop of Rome, he writes that so much attention was devoted to the relation between collegiality and primacy that the principle of collegiality itself had been obscured, particularly its foundation in the structure of the early Church.

Thus he underlines, from an ecumenical perspective, the importance of the rediscovery of the local church, much discussed in the second session, showing that the one Church exists as a plurality of churches, with "[e]ach local community assembled with its bishop around the table of the Lord," united in communion with each other and with the bishop of Rome. He rejected Professor Edmund Schlink's view that all the separated churches are equally legitimate manifestations of the Church; instead he said that one hopes for the hour "when 'the Churches' that exist outside 'the Church' will enter into its unity," or as he would say today, when the other "Churches and ecclesial communities" enter into full communion with the one Church. Evident here in Ratzinger's discussion is the eucharistic ecclesiology, based on the concept of *koinonia* or communion, that would prove so fruitful in the decades after the Council.

The Church in the Modern World

Ratzinger has long been critical of the Pastoral Constitution on the Church in the Modern World, *Gaudium et spes*. In his 1982 *Theologische Prinzipienlehre*, he questioned its pre-theological concept of "world," its emphasis on dialogue as a mutual search for solutions, its "astonishing optimism," and the apparent lack of an "attitude of critical reserve toward forces that have left their imprint on the modern world."[4] He had made similar comments immediately after the Council in the present book. The text of *Gaudium et spes*, originally called Schema 13, was drafted in French. Its "chief architect" was the German Redemptorist Bernard Häring. Although the text was intended to be biblical in its approach rather than scholastic and philosophical, Ratzinger found it "neither biblically precise nor really in line with modern thought." He commended its attempt to speak to modern men and women without the specialized language or jargon of theology, but thought that the text left out what was proper to the work of Christ or the message of the Church, opting instead for dialogue, as though faith were "a kind of recondite philosophy." For Ratzinger that meant acting as though faith had nothing to say that touched the heart of human existence. Influenced by Teilhard de Chardin, the text of the constitution seemed to identify

Christian hope with progress through technological development, revealing "an almost naïve progressive optimism." But this overlooked the Christian message of Christ's victory through the cross: "Thus Christianity cannot mean a sacral transfiguration of the technological. Rather, it reveals a realm which the technological cannot redeem."

With this as background to the debate on the text, Ratzinger moves to consider several complex problems among those taken up by the constitution. Its approach was somewhat tentative, offering "comprehensive orientations" without giving definitive answers. First, he considers the text's treatment of the Christian in an increasingly technological world. Pointing to a new historical situation, in which technology has given humans new power over the world, thus leading to an increasing unification of humankind (no. 33), the constitution stressed that the Christian message should move people to the building up of the world and service of others (no. 34). Recognizing the limited competence of the Church in secular matters, it developed "an explicit doctrine on the autonomy of the secular." But progress remains ambivalent; technology cannot decode the meaning of existence, which is where the properly Christian sphere comes into view.

Second, Ratzinger's review of the constitution's teaching on marriage and the family (nos. 47–52) is particularly interesting, especially in light of ongoing debates in moral theology today. To provide the background for the constitution's treatment, he argues that with the New Testament lacking a developed moral teaching, early Christianity relied heavily on classical antiquity and especially Stoicism for its ethical norms. What resulted was the traditional Catholic "generative" view of marriage. Stoicism's naturalistic approach made marriage subordinate to the human race as a whole and thus to procreation. It saw the overriding moral norm as acting "according to nature," the effect of which was to relegate marriage chiefly to the biological level. Ratzinger speaks of "the great significance" of the fact that neither the concept of the "prime end of procreation," nor the concept of marital behavior "according to nature," has any place in the pastoral constitution. While reaffirming the social significance of marriage, he speaks of the "decided difference" between moral statements based on concepts of race, propagation, and being in accordance with nature, and another view that focuses on the Word of God, on responsibility toward children and spouse, and on the community of humankind.

The third example is the constitution's teaching on war and peace (nos. 87–92). It approaches the question as a moral dilemma that the traditional "just war" doctrine did not resolve. Without issuing unequivocal directives on the use of modern weapons, it repeated recent condemnations of the indiscriminate destruction of cities or regions and argued that "the attempt must be made to approach as closely as possible what is morally desirable." Thus the goal must be a total peace that converts swords into plowshares, doing whatever contributes toward this end.

Ratzinger concludes that the constitution, despite its vagueness on these questions, is good because it seeks to do the possible, not the impossible. It does not attempt to establish timeless norms for complex questions. In recognizing what may be "licit" only as a concession, and far from what is truly right, it points the way beyond merely secular considerations to a recognition of our unrighteousness and our need for God, and thus to the very heart of Christianity.

Two schemas were taken up in one of the last months of the Council. The schema on missions attempted to give a new rationale for missionary activity in the context of the prevailing idea that God can save people even though they are outside the Church. Acknowledging the importance of what we today call contextual theologies, Ratzinger noted that Christianity had not really been implanted in Asia, where conversion, in the absence of a genuine Asian Christianity, has meant so far practically conversion to Europeanism. The schema on the priestly ministry and life changed the one-sided emphasis on the idea of priesthood as sacrifice to the idea of priesthood as service to the faith. Noting that the pope had forbidden debate on priestly celibacy, Ratzinger observed that in view of the shortage of priests the Church could not avoid reviewing this question quietly without evading its responsibility to preach the Gospel within the context of our times.

On October 28, after a recess of eight days, the Council passed the Decree on the Pastoral Office of Bishops in the Church, the Decree on the Renewal of Religious Life, the Decree on Priestly Training, the Decree on Christian Education, and the Declaration on the Relation of the Church to the non-Christian Religions. The last four texts were approved on December 7: the Pastoral Constitution on the Church in the Modern World, the Decree on the Ministry and Life of Priests, the Decree on the Church's Missionary Activity, and the Declaration on Religious Liberty.

Conclusion

All Ratzinger's acuity is evident in this postconciliar report. In observing that it was "as never before unmistakably clear that the Church had become an international Church," no longer dependent on European leadership, he anticipated Rahner's remark thirteen years later that the Council represented the transformation of Western Christianity into a world Church.[5] The Synod of Bishops should have been a step toward such an international Church with an international episcopate exercising real authority. But it has not worked out that way. Pope Paul VI announced the creation of the synod in his address of September 14, 1965. As the *motu proprio* the next day made clear, the synod was "directly and immediately subordinated to the authority of the bishop of Rome." Noting the differences between the synod as conceived by the Council and its eventual realization, Ratzinger repeats the comment that a collegial organ had been turned into an instrument of the primacy. Though he tried to put a positive spin on this, suggesting that the synod's subordination to the pope would keep it from being subordinated to the curia, it is the latter situation that has in fact resulted. In later years he would argue that making the synod a central governing agency would lead to more burdensome centralism than that of the curia.

In his preface to the English edition, he says that his book represents not the detached view of the historian but rather "the account of a personal journey through the landscape of each session, with an open view toward future developments." This last comment is worth noting. Throughout the book, he stresses that we may speak of the Council as a new beginning; that its texts are not

THEOLOGICAL HIGHLIGHTS OF VATICAN II

meant to save work for theologians, but rather should stimulate it and open new horizons; that much remains incomplete and fragmentary, a beginning more than an end; that its real importance will be achieved only when it is translated into the everyday life of the Church. Even when, almost forty years later as pope, he contrasted "a hermeneutic of discontinuity and rupture" with a "hermeneutic of reform," he stresses that the true spirit of the Council is not found in contrasts between the preconciliar and postconciliar Church or in false interpretations of conciliar compromises made in search of unanimity, suggesting that the "old things" are now pointless. The true spirit of the Council is found "in the impulses toward the new that are contained in the texts."[6]

—Thomas P. Rausch, SJ
T. Marie Chilton Professor of Catholic Theology
Loyola Marymount University, Los Angeles, California

Notes to Introduction

1. Joseph Ratzinger, *Milestones: Memoirs 1927–1977* (San Francisco: Ignatius Press, 1998), 57.

2. See Jared Wicks, "Six Texts by Prof. Joseph Ratzinger as *peritus* before and during Vatican Council II," *Gregorianum* 89/2 (2008): 233–311.

3. *History of Vatican II, Vol. III*, ed. Giuseppe Alberigo, English version ed. Joseph A. Komonchak

(Maryknoll, NY: Orbis Press, 2000), 113; the text in *LG* reads "in virtue of the sacramental consecration and by hierarchical communion with the head and members of the college" (Flannery translation).

4. See Joseph Ratzinger, *Principles of Catholic Theology* (San Francisco: Ignatius Press, 1987), 379–80. Karl Rahner, who also worked on *GS*, found its undertone "too euphoric in its evaluation of humanity and the human condition," insisting that human endeavors often wind up in blind alleys, including those of the Church; *Theological Investigations*, Vol. 22 (New York: Crossroad, 1991), 158.

5. Karl Rahner, "Towards a Fundamental Theological Interpretation of Vatican Council II," *Theological Studies* 40 (1979), 718.

6. Pope Benedict XVI, "Address of his Holiness Benedict XVI to the Roman Curia Offering Them his Christmas Greetings," December 22, 2005, www.vatican.va.

PART ONE

The First Session

I

OPENING OF THE COUNCIL AND ELECTION OF THE COMMISSIONS

Signal to first the periods decisions

As we look at the Council in retrospect, one thing is certain. There was at the start a certain discomforting feeling that the whole enterprise might come to nothing more than a mere rubber-stamping of decisions already made, thus impeding rather than fostering the renewal needed in the Catholic Church. Had this happened, the Council would have disappointed and discouraged all those who had placed their hopes in it; it would have paralyzed all their healthy dynamism and swept aside once again the many new questions people of our era had put to the Church.

The preparatory commissions had undoubtedly worked hard, but their diligence was somewhat distressing. Seventy schemata had been produced, enough to fill 2,000 pages of folio size. This was more than double the quantity of texts produced by all previous councils put together. How were the fathers to wade through this verbal wilderness? How was the Council to distill from all this material a message meaningful and intelligible to contemporary man? Was it not much more likely that the Council would ultimately issue a fearsome kind of dogmatic super-compendium which would weigh down upon any future work like a heavy millstone?

Yet there was a certain feeling of exhilaration at the opening of the Council in Rome, the mysterious sense of new beginnings that has a way of stirring man and propelling him forward. This was even more true in that here one could feel the imminence of an event of historic significance. The diversity of tongues (even more tongues than are usually heard in Rome), the prospect of rich new encounters, the promise of what was coming—all this made one forget for the moment the secret anxieties he had, so to speak, stuffed in his luggage when he left for the Council. This strange ambivalence of feeling was there at the opening cere-monies in St. Peter's. The mighty basilica, the grandeur of the ancient liturgy, the colorful diversity of the visi-tors from all over the world—all this was magnificently impressive. Yet there was, on the other hand, an unde-niable uneasiness, whose most obvious symptom was annoyance with the endlessly long ceremonies. This was surely no objective criterion, but it did reveal something deeper: namely, that the opening liturgy

liturgy

did not really involve all who were present, and it had little inner coherence. Did it make sense for 2,500 bishops, not to mention the other faithful there, to be relegated to the role of mere spectators at a ceremony in which only the celebrants and the Sistine Choir had a voice? Was not the fact that the active participation of those present was not required symptomatic of a wrong that needed remedy? And why did the Credo have to be repeated after Mass, when the Mass itself contains a profession of faith? What was the need for an ornate additional liturgy of the Word, when the Mass itself contained appropriate epistle and gospel messages? Why were long litanies sung outside the Mass, when the liturgy of the Mass itself provided for the insertion of suitable intercessory prayers? Two distinct liturgies had over the years been unrelatedly juxtaposed, painfully revealing the dangerous archaism which had come to enshroud the Mass since Trent, so that the real meaning of its various parts was no longer intelligible. People no longer realized that the enthronement of the gospel, the profession of faith and intercessory prayers were actually contained in the Mass itself.

Yet no observer could fail to notice how different the liturgical ceremonies at the close of the first session were from the opening-day ceremonies. This was a sign of the success of the Council. At the concluding Mass on December 8, 1962, the responses and other fixed parts were sung in unison by the bishops and all those present. This was the result of the bishops' own initiative.

Then, too, there were positive aspects even in the opening ceremony. One of these was the address of Pope John in which he disavowed all merely negative condemnations and asked instead that the Council apply the medicine of compassion. The Council was not to engage in scholastic disputation, arguing fine points of specific doctrines. Rather their efforts were to be directed toward a fundamental renewal of the universal Church, in living dialogue with the present time and its needs. Perhaps even more impressive was a small gesture, received with special gratitude by the participants from the Churches of the East. The pope signed his confession of faith, "John, Bishop of the Catholic Church." No pretentious titles; just the simple official designation which united him with his brethren, the bishops of the universal Church of God.

But on the next day, when all attention was focused on the first general congregation, the uneasiness reappeared again. The fathers' first task was the election of commission members. But how was this to be approached? Suddenly a phenomenon which had hitherto gone unnoticed made its impact—the fact that in the Catholic Church, although there were strong, unifying bonds between the individual bishops and Rome, there were hardly any "horizontal" ties

THEOLOGICAL HIGHLIGHTS OF VATICAN II

among the bishops themselves. These really should have constituted an essential element of Catholicity. Yet often enough even bishops of the same country did not know one another, and international contacts were only accidental and exceptional. How then could one vote when no one knew anyone else? How could anyone draw votes outside his own national episcopate? But wider strength was needed for the requisite majority. It seemed that the 2,500 fathers were hopelessly incapable of coordinated accomplishment.

The fathers, of course, had a comparatively easy way out. They could reelect the members of the preparatory commissions appointed by the pope, thus dispensing with all effort and labor. It seems that the curia had counted on such a solution. Thus the first sensation of the Council came in the general congregation of October 13 when Cardinals Liénart and Frings arose and demanded a postponement of the election scheduled for that day so that the bishops might first get a chance to know one another and thus be able to hold a meaningful election. The fact that this proposal met with a lively ovation, despite the official prohibition against applause, indicated that a decision of great moment had here been made. The Council had shown its resolve to act independently and autonomously, rather than be degraded to the status of a mere executive organ of the preparatory commissions.

[handwritten: horizontal]

Hence the initial uneasiness had produced something quite positive. In the following days extensive contacts were initiated among the various bishops' conferences. The result was a number of different lists of candidates. The one worked out by the central European group was distinguished by its broad international character, and thus was able to draw the greatest number of votes. Out of the distress of the hour, then, something really new and needed had come back—the development of a "horizontal Catholicity," with cross-connections among those who call themselves Catholic. Yves Congar had stressed such bonds as a necessary complementary element to the "vertical" unity joining all to the center of the Church. For, as the start of the Council had shown, these horizontal connections had actually been lost in the Church's practical life.

A second decision had been made in what had seemed a mere technical resolution. The Council had taken a giant step beyond being a mere sounding board for propaganda. It had decisively assumed the function assigned it by canon law—the exercise of supreme power over the entire Church.

Still another important result of this decision by the Council was that, in this independent body of bishops, the curia found a force to reckon with and a real partner in discussion. Previously it had seemed that Roman officialdom was the only really formative and

[handwritten: Church & bishops]

active authority in the Church, and that apart from the curia there was really nothing but non-authoritative outsiders. Now it became clear that, besides the official curia organs (subordinated to the pope), the body of bishops was a reality in its own right, infusing into the dialogue and the very life of the Church its own spiritual experience. Such a reality obviously could not have come into being overnight. Rather, a long dormant spiritual power was now coming into the open. What had happened during previous decades in fraternal dialogue with separated Christians, in the struggle with the world of atheism, and in the Church's own spiritual awakening from country to country—all this experience was in this moment distilled into an effective force. One could feel more strongly than ever before that apparently ineffectual encounters and events, which we had sometimes resignedly written off as useless, had actually been working in the Church, and had now emerged as a factor in its life.

Besides the initiation of a living "horizontal Catholicity," we may consider, as a product of this first basic Council decision, the restoration of a fruitful interplay between periphery and center, between the living multiplicity of Catholic life (represented by the episcopacy) and the unity which the primacy must protect. And we might add that the interplay between these two elements is not what a puzzled observer might easily have thought it to be—a kind of embarrassing break-down in the Church. This interplay, the result of mutual stimulation between multiplicity and unity, was rather part of the Church's vital self-fulfillment. All living realities demand just such a dynamic tension within themselves.

Which groups of bishops most contributed to this new episcopal dynamism? From external indications, we might single out three groups. First the central European bishops (Germany, France, Holland, and Belgium), second, the bishops of South America, and third, the mission bishops. Initially more reserved were the Anglo-Saxon group (England, Ireland and the United States). The Spanish bishops were opening up to new issues. Most reserved were the Italian bishops, who had still not come to see themselves as having their own power independently of the curia. Because of various historical traditions, they saw themselves as largely subordinated to it.

This more superficial lining up of episcopal groups indicates that the differences of attitude were only in small part explicable in terms of variant national traditions. The bishops' varying attitudes were partly due to historical differences and partly due to variant kinds of encounter with the spiritual needs of the present age. The strongest initiatives came from bishops of regions marked by religious pluralism, and thus in close contact

Cause for pushing

with the problems of separated Christianity, as well as from bishops who, because of their direct confrontation with modern atheism, felt challenged to present the response of faith in a new way.

Nor do we read too much into the first day's decision when we see a fourth result in it. In that decision we could already sense what Pope John was soon after to call "the holy freedom of the Council." The atmosphere of the Council was predetermined by the generous spirit of this pope, who in this markedly differed from the pope (Pius IX) who had called Vatican Council I. Without saying much, Pope John, by the influence of his personality, encouraged the Council to openness and candor. We shall have occasion later to show in more detail how the anti-Modernistic neurosis which had again and again crippled the Church since the turn of the century here seemed to be approaching a cure. Here there emerged a new awareness of how the Church could conduct a dialogue in fraternal frankness without violating the obedience that belongs to faith.

The results of the elections confirmed the above-mentioned indications. The bishops who were most likely to carry forward the initiatives of the first general congregation were precisely the ones who received the vast majority of votes. Thus the Council in those early days had already set its fundamental course, a course which in subsequent sessions was somewhat inaccurately described as "pastoral" and "ecumenical." What this means will be more closely specified in what follows.

II

FIRST DEBATES ON THE LITURGY SCHEMA

The "Message of the Council Fathers to Mankind," issued on October 20, did not properly constitute an act of the Council. It was simply a joint statement of all the bishops of the world to the faithful everywhere and to humanity at large. The actual work of the Council began with the schema on the liturgy on Monday, October 21, 1962. Out of some 70 prepared schemata, seven had been submitted to the fathers in printed form a few weeks prior to the opening of the Council. They had the following titles: On the Sources of Revelation; On the Preservation in Purity of the Deposit of Faith; On Morality; On Marriage and Virginity; On the Sacred Liturgy; On Modern Means of Communication; On the Unity of the Church. It was clear that the first four schemata, worked out by Cardinal Ottaviani's theological commission, would trigger real conflict, and that the last two had not been fully worked out. Thus the often repeated wish of the fathers polled before the Council: Begin with the question of liturgical reform. The presidents who were responsible for arranging the daily order complied with this request. This turned out to be a fortunate decision, for this text was both carefully balanced and courageous, and so the fathers were able to begin with a positive text which had wide implications for the future. This inspired optimism, and gave the progressive elements a chance to unite at the very beginning on a positive project. It would have been much more difficult to unite in an effort of negative criticism. Here constructive, forward-looking work could be done. The hesitant could be carried along because the draft itself made clear that what was at issue here was not negative or destructive criticism, but rather greater fullness. The proposed text offered an answer to questions which had long troubled the missionary bishops. This text was complete enough to be a perfect basis for debate, yet it was open enough to leave room for questions. Therefore, in debating it the Council would be able to express its own mind; it could find itself spiritually; and above all, it could experiment with procedural forms.

The problem of procedure was very real. After all, a total of 2,900 fathers—bishops, auxiliary bishops, abbots and superiors of orders—were entitled to take part. Of these, 2,540 had attended the opening meeting. Although the number subsequently decreased to about 2,000, this still remained a distressingly large total for a deliberative body. Added to this was the fact that few of the fathers present had any parliamentary or synodal experience, and that all were only in the process of getting acquainted. So it becomes clear what great difficulties the assembly faced. It was simply unimaginable how such a vast body of men would be able to achieve results. Council rules which restricted each speaker to ten minutes (later eight) and required prior written application were obviously an inadequate remedy. Various proposals were made: to form an electoral body, proportioned to the size of the national episcopates, with delegates chosen by these episcopates; to form various parties. Both suggestions were rejected by the Council. And in retrospect we can say that the Council was well-advised to reject them. It was precisely this real if slightly cumbersome catholicity of the assemblage which was, historically speaking, to be so decisive. This catholicity would only have been jeopardized by reducing its diversity. The fact that no parties were formed indicated a sense of responsibility toward truth. No Council can allow the individual to be subsumed under some kind of party; each person must be responsible only to his conscience and his theological convictions. Moreover, the formation of parties would have meant the risk of a division along national lines. The only possible solution, as became increasingly obvious in the course of the liturgy debate, was the *ad hoc* formation of alignments on specific issues. Here those who agreed in one opinion could join in representing their cause, and thus focus the overall Council effort. Another improvement was the amending of the Council rules to permit the presidium to terminate debate and thus limit possibly endless filibustering.

Let us return to our original point. The decision to begin with the liturgy schema was not merely a technically correct move. Its significance went far deeper. This decision was a profession of faith in what is truly central to the Church—the ever renewed marriage of the Church with her Lord, actualized in the eucharistic mystery where the Church, participating in the sacrifice of Jesus Christ, fulfills its innermost mission, the adoration of the triune God. Beyond all the superficially more important issues, there was here a profession of faith in the true source of the Church's life, and the proper point of departure for all renewal. The text did not restrict itself to mere changes in individual rubrics, but was inspired from this profound perspective of faith. The text implied an entire ecclesiology and thus anticipated (in a degree that cannot be too highly appreciated) the main theme of the entire Council—its teaching on the Church. Thus the Church was freed from the "hierarchical narrowness" of the previous hundred years, and returned to its sacramental origins. Finally, the Council was here able to reap the harvest that had been ripening in the Church's difficult struggle during recent decades.

No need here to discuss the details of liturgical reform. Rather, we will have done enough if we can highlight a few of the basic tendencies that left their imprint on the entire text.

(1) We should first mention the return to Christian origins and the pruning of certain accretions often enough concealing the original liturgical nucleus. The priority of the Sunday liturgy over saints' days had to be restored because of the connection between Sunday and Easter. Mystery had to be restored to priority over devotion, and simple structure had to replace the rampant overgrowth of forms. The return to sources was to have its effect especially in the Mass liturgy. Ritual rigidity, which almost obliterated the meaning of individual actions, had to be defrosted. The liturgy of the Word had to be restored: the proclamation of the Word of God once more had to call and speak to man. The dialogical nature of the whole liturgical celebration and its essence as the common service of the People of God had to be once more fully

emphasized. The natural consequence of this was a reduction of the status of private Masses in favor of emphasis on greater communal participation. This is expressed in the text by the lapidary sentence: "The celebration of Mass with public participation is to be preferred." Concelebration is thus encouraged. Two other tendencies are involved in what has just been pointed out.

Participation

(2) There is and will be a stronger emphasis on the Word as an element of equal value with sacrament. The text says about this: "The treasures of the bible are to be opened up more lavishly, so that richer fare may be provided for the faithful at the table of God's Word. In this way a more representative portion of the sacred scriptures will be read to the people.…The homily, therefore, is to be highly esteemed as a part of the liturgy itself; in fact, at those Masses celebrated with the assistance of the people on Sundays and feasts of obligation, it should not be omitted.…" (*Constitution on the Sacred Liturgy*, nn. 51-52). There is also to be a new arrangement of biblical readings to make the treasures of scripture more liturgically accessible than before.

Word & Sacrament

homily

(3) A special objective of liturgical reform, as was mentioned above, was a more active par-

ticipation of the laity, the inclusion of the whole communion of God into a holy fulfillment. A sign in which we can clearly see the scope of this is the provision made now for the laity to communicate in certain cases under both species.

(4) An especially important development is the decentralization of the liturgical decision-making. The first chapter of the *Constitution on the Sacred Liturgy* contains a statement that represents for the Latin Church a fundamental innovation. The formulation of liturgical laws for their own regions is now, within limits, the responsibility of the various conferences of bishops. And this is not by delegation from the Holy See, but by virtue of their own independent authority. This decision makes it possible to restore to the liturgy that catholicity which the Church fathers saw symbolized in Psalm 44—the bride with her many-colored raiment. We may restore to the liturgy all the fullness which is quickening the Church. At the same time something of importance in its ecclesial significance is also involved. One should consider that from the standpoint of canon law the bishops' conferences as such did not exist before. They possessed no leg-

islative power but were merely advisory. Now that they possess in their own right a definite legislative function, they appear as a new element in the Church's structure and form a kind of quasi-synodal agency between individual bishops and the pope. In this way a kind of continuing synodal element is built into the Church, and thereby the college of bishops assumes a new function. Perhaps one could say that this small paragraph, which for the first time assigns to the conferences of bishops their own canonical authority, has more significance for the theology of the episcopacy and for the long desired strengthening of episcopal power than anything in the *Constitution on the Church* itself. For in this case an accomplished fact is involved, and facts, as history teaches, carry more weight than pure doctrine. And so, without fanfare, and largely unnoticed by the public, the Council had produced a work fundamental in the renewal of ecclesiology.

(5) The subject that preempted by far the most discussion time during the first session was, oddly enough, the debate over the language of the liturgy. If one considers, however, that the Constitution *Veterum sapientia*

had appeared shortly before and showed a significant predilection for the Latin language, then one can well understand the sharply drawn battle lines. Then, too, there was the force of more than 1,500 years' tradition. The discussion did not lack color. It was not uncommon that glowing panegyrics in favor of Latin were themselves delivered in labored pidgin Latin, while the most forceful advocates of the vernacular could express themselves in classical Latin. The strangest proposal was that of Cardinal Spellman who wanted no concessions made to the vernacular in the Mass, yet expressed the wish that priests be allowed to say their breviaries in the vernacular. To show that the discussions could, however, produce profound insights we wish to quote from the speech of the Melchite Patriarch Maximos Saigh:

"It appears to me that the almost absolute value which is attributed to the Latin language in the liturgy, in instruction and in the administration of the Latin Church presents a kind of anomaly for the Eastern Church; for without doubt Christ spoke to his contemporaries in their own language. He used a language which was understandable to all his hearers, namely Aramaic, when he celebrated the first eucharistic sacrifice. The apostles and disciples acted likewise. It would never have occurred to them that the celebrant in a Christian assembly should read the passages of scripture, should sing the psalms, should preach or break the bread, using a different language than that of the congregation. Paul himself says explicitly: 'If you bless with the spirit [i.e., in an unintelligible language], how is one who is present as an outsider to say "Amen" to your thanksgiving when he does not understand what you are saying? You may give thanks well enough, but the other is not edified....In church I should prefer to speak five words with my mind, in order to instruct others, than ten thousand words in [unintelligible] tongues' (1 Cor. 14, 16-19). All the reasons one can bring forward in favor of the untouchability of Latin—a liturgical language but a dead one—must give way before this clear, unequivocal and precise reasoning of the Apostle. The Latin language is dead, but the Church remains alive. So, too, the language which mediates grace and the Holy Spirit must also be a living language since it is intended for men and not for angels. No language can be untouchable...."

Only if we consider how deeply the meaning of language pervades man's activity—and that language is

language matters, liturgy & theol & phil

not merely an external, superficial and accidental thing, but is rather the incarnation of the human spirit which thinks and lives in its very speech—only then can we judge the extent of the change inaugurated in the liturgical debates. And so, the rigor and the detail of the debate were ultimately justified. The decision over language was of great importance, and thus had to be carefully and tactfully worked out. Only then could such a program really assist the new confrontation between the Christian spirit and the modern spirit. For it can hardly be denied that the sterility to which Catholic theology and philosophy had in many ways been doomed since the end of the Enlightenment was due not least to a language in which the living choices of the human spirit no longer found a place. Theology often bypassed new ideas, was not enriched by them and remained unable to transform them.

The words of Patriarch Maximos give us a chance to digress somewhat on the structure of the Council. We should consider once more the full assembly that gathered daily in St. Peter's. Alongside Latin bishops from all over the world, the representatives of the different Uniate Churches of the East also took their places. History has said much about whether the Uniate Churches are good or bad. Sometimes it has been said with good reason that the Uniates were more of a barrier than a bridge to the Orthodox. However

THEOLOGICAL HIGHLIGHTS OF VATICAN II

that may be, during Vatican Council II the union of Eastern rite Churches to the Catholic Church proved to be of the utmost positive value. For the East was present in these Churches, with its own voice and vote as an inner corrective to Latin exclusivity. The East was able again and again to open up the narrow Latin horizon and to force the Council to think not in a Latin but in a catholic manner, and to avoid the fateful equating of Catholicity with Latinity.

Besides the fathers there were present in the Council hall two silent but no less effective groups: the almost 200 *periti* named by the pope, and the non-Catholic observers. Their presence was a new and highly fruitful element. Without saying a word, they created an atmosphere; no one could speak without being aware of their presence. This gave the words of any speaker a special ecumenical weight. The distressing urgency of divided Christendom was ever present in the Council hall and left its mark on the efforts of the assembly. We hardly need mention what it meant to us when representatives of Churches, which often enough viewed Catholicism with prejudice and mistrust, were actually able to experience the Catholic Church directly. They felt the vitality and frankness which are so much a part of the faith and the Catholic Church.

The liturgical debate that many thought had dragged on too long ended on November 14, 1962, with a vote for the basic adoption of the schema, with the necessary changes left up to the commission. Even the optimists could not have expected the result of the voting—2,162 in favor, 46 opposed (with 7 invalid votes). And so the adoption was a decision that both looked to the future and showed encouragingly that the forces of renewal were stronger than anyone would have dared hope.

III

EARLY DEBATE ON REVELATION

The Council faced a more difficult situation when, on the same day, the schema dealing with "the sources of revelation" was presented to the fathers. The text was, if one may use the label, utterly a product of the "anti-Modernist" mentality that had taken shape about the turn of the century. The text was written in a spirit of condemnation and negation which, in contrast with the great positive initiative of the liturgy schema, had a frigid and even offensive tone to many of the fathers. And this despite the fact that the content of the text was new to no one. It was exactly like dozens of textbooks familiar to the bishops from their seminary days; and in some cases their former professors were actually responsible for the text now presented to them.

In order to understand the intellectual mentality behind this text, it is necessary to recall the embattled atmosphere of the Church during the previous hundred years. This atmosphere is first clearly marked in the Syllabus of Pius IX (1864) in which the Church decisively and uncompromisingly detached itself from the growing error of the "modern mind." As with every historical necessity, however, it undoubtedly went about this with excessively one-sided zeal. This development reaches its zenith in the various measures of Pius X against Modernism (the decree *Lamentabili* and the encyclical *Pascendi* [1907], and, finally, the "oath against Modernism" [1910]). During these years there arose an embittered discussion that found expression in such tragic figures as Loisy and Tyrrell, men who thought they could not save the faith without throwing away the inner core along with the expendable shell. Such figures and their tragic schizophrenia show forth the mortal danger that threatened Catholicism at the first outbreak of the modern mind. They explain Pius X's uncompromising opposition to the spirit of novelty which was stirring everywhere. It must be said that, in sifting it out, much real wheat was lost along with the chaff. This historical perspective helps explain, then, that secret fear and mistrust of any theological expression of modern historical and philosophical thought. This same anxiety persisted until its last reverberation sounded in the encyclical *Humani generis* of Pius XII. This document pursued once more the line of thought of Pius IX and Pius X.

The schemata of the theological commission, the first of which now lay before the fathers for consideration, breathed this same spirit. The same cramped thinking, once so necessary as a line of defense, impregnated the text and informed it with a theology of negations and prohibitions, although in themselves they might well have been valid, they certainly could not produce that positive note which was now to be expected from the Council. In any case, none of this could appear strange or startling to the bishops. Familiar with the origins of these opinions and aware of the struggles they themselves had been through, they found it easy to recognize in the text the very sentiments many of them had brought to the Council. But everything that had happened since the Council began had basically changed the situation. The bishops were no longer the same men they had been before the Council. First of all, they had discovered themselves as an episcopate, with their own powers and their own collective responsibility. Secondly, the passage of the liturgy schema had given rise to a new possibility foreign to the old pattern of "anti-ism" and negativity, the possibility of abandoning the defensive and really undertaking a Christian "offensive." They could now think and act in a positive manner. The spark was ignited. The words of Pope John's opening speech now acquired meaning, became understandable. He had insisted that the Church was no longer to condemn but rather to dispense the medicine of compassion, that the Council was not to speak negatively but to present the faith in a new and positive way, and finally that the Council must refrain from pronouncing anathemas. These very words, previously considered as an expression of the pope's personal temperament, words that had puzzled many, now made sense. And so it could happen that, without prior agreement, Cardinals Liénart, Frings, Léger, König, Alfrink, Suenens, Ritter and Bea, each from his own point of view, delivered sharp criticisms of the schema, something surprising to both its authors and its opponents.

What was the central issue? Among the theological questions open to serious discussion were the relationship of scripture to tradition and the way in which faith is related to history. Also under discussion was a proper understanding of inspiration and of the historicity of events narrated in scripture. The whole question which contemporary historical scholarship raised, and which was postponed rather than solved by Modernism, stood open once more to debate. Beyond these specific questions dealing with the interpretation of faith which cannot be treated here in detail, there was at issue a more fundamental conflict of attitudes of mind that amounted to more than a mere quarrel about theological differences. The real question behind the discussion could be put this way: Was the intellectual position of "anti-Modernism"—the old policy of exclusiveness, condemnation and defense leading to an almost neurotic denial of all that was new—to be continued? Or would the Church, after it had taken all the necessary precautions to protect the faith, turn over a new leaf and move on into a new and positive encounter with its own origins, with its brothers and with the world of today? Since a clear majority of the fathers opted for the second alternative, we may even speak of the Council as a new beginning. We may also say that with this decision there was a major advance over Vatican Council I. Both Trent and Vatican Council I set up bulwarks for the faith to assure it and to protect it; Vatican Council II turned itself to a new task, building on the work of the two previous Councils.

Two main arguments were used to defend the new position. They rested upon the intention of Pope John that the texts should be pastoral and their theology ecumenical. It must be granted that both arguments employed by the progressive interests at the

THEOLOGICAL IIIGHLIGHTS OF VATICAN II

Council are open to misinterpretation. They can in fact be unobjective, open to misunderstanding and ambiguity. What they did mean, and the sense in which they were actually used under given circumstances, may well be surmised from what we have thus far said. "Pastoral" should not mean nebulous, without substance, merely "edifying"—meanings sometimes given to it. Rather what was meant was positive care for the man of today who is not helped by condemnations and who has been told for too long what is false and what he may not do. Modern man really wishes to hear what is true. He has, indeed, not heard enough truth, enough of the positive message of faith for our own time, enough of what the faith has to say to our age. "Pastoral" should not mean something vague and imprecise, but rather something free from wrangling, and free also from entanglement in questions that concern scholars alone. It should imply openness to the possibility of discussion in a time which calls for new responses and new obligations. "Pastoral" should mean, finally, speaking in the language of scripture, of the early Church Fathers, and of contemporary man. Technical theological language has its purpose and is indeed necessary, but it does not belong in the kerygma and in our confession of faith.

"Ecumenical" must not mean concealing truth so as not to displease others. What is true must be said openly and without concealment; full truth is part of full love. "Ecumenical" must mean that we cease seeing others as mere adversaries against whom we must defend ourselves. We have pursued such a course long enough. "Ecumenical" means that we must try to recognize as brothers, with whom we can speak and from whom we can also learn, those who do not share our views. "Ecumenical" must mean that we give proper attention to the truth which another has, and to another's serious Christian concern in a matter in which he differs from us, or even errs. "Ecumenical" means to consider the whole, and not to single out some partial aspect that calls for condemnation or correction. "Ecumenical" means that we present the inner totality of our faith in order to make known to our separated brothers that Catholicism clearly contains all that is truly Christian. "Ecumenical" and "Catholic" in their very etymology say the same thing. Therefore, to be a Catholic is not to become entangled in separatism, but to be open to the fullness of Christianity. It was precisely this attitude which the fathers had to assert against the proposed text. The texts almost exclusively relied upon the Latin theology of the last hundred years in continuation of the fight against Modernism, and in so doing these texts were obviously threatened by a narrowness in which the wide scope of Catholicism could scarcely be detected. It is clear, therefore, from what we have said about the very basic division of mind involved in the revelation schema, that in subsequent debates important specific details of the schema were of comparatively secondary importance. It is also clear that in the fathers' debates there was no fundamental division of dogmatic viewpoint; there was rather an important difference in the basic spiritual approach to the problem of how the Church was to meet its present responsibilities. The voting on November 20 proved that the great majority of the Council opted for the positive position and had made up its mind to abandon an outmoded negative defensiveness.

As the press made abundantly clear, the question to be voted on was so worded that for the moment the issue was obfuscated. According to normal procedure the schema would have been presented to the fathers to pass or reject; two-thirds of all the votes would have been required for passage, while a good one-third would have been sufficient to kill the schema. But instead the Council was asked to vote whether the present schema should be *withdrawn* or not. Now the text's opponents had the burden of mustering two-thirds of the vote, and a good one-third was quite enough to save the schema. The result is well known: 1,368 of the fathers voted for the withdrawal of the schema—in other words, opposed the text—while 813 voted for keeping the schema.

Another 100 votes or so would have provided the two-thirds necessary to kill the schema. Thus only about one-third of the fathers had voted for the proposed text. Nevertheless, this device had saved the schema despite the fact that quite obviously it ran counter to the will of the majority. The deep dismay and even anger that resulted dissolved on the following day when the pope himself set aside the text of the schema and turned it over to a mixed commission, headed by Cardinals Ottaviani and Bea, for thorough revision. Thus the will of the majority was carried out. The pope had asserted his authority in favor of the Council majority. This decision was obviously of great fundamental importance. The Council had resolutely set itself against perpetuating a one-sided anti-Modernism and so had chosen a new and positive approach. In this sense, we may consider November 20 or November 21, 1962, as a real turning point. It was a turning point, too, in the sense that, in contrast to Trent and Vatican Council I, the pope had rejected curial dominance and sided with the Council.

IV

LAST PHASE OF
THE FIRST SESSION

With the majority vote of November 20 and its authoritative reinforcement the next day, the basic decision of the first session was made. Compared to this, everything else in the first session appears derivative and supplementary. Therefore, we can treat the rest of the business of this session with relative brevity.

Let us first consider the other individual achievements. (1) The preface and first chapter of the liturgy schema were passed in the final form worked out by the commissions. These texts, together with the remaining parts of the schema, had only to be accepted in a public session presided over by the pope to become law. (2) The schema on the media of communications (press, film, radio and television) was discussed. The Council, though it declared its agreement with the principles developed, expressed the wish that the text be radically condensed and that details be left to a pastoral instruction to be prepared later with the help of specialists from various nations. (3) The schema on the unity of the Church, worked out by the commission for the Eastern Church, was discussed. The

49

Council agreed to integrate this text (which dealt only with the Eastern Churches) with the corresponding text prepared by Cardinal Bea's secretariat and with the chapter on ecumenism of the schema on the Church. For this purpose, the Council returned these texts to the respective commissions. (4) Discussion of the schema on the Church was initiated. A proposal by Cardinal Ottaviani to deal first with the schema on the Mother of God did not win the necessary majority. Although in the discussion on the Church a number of important points had been made which again confirmed the openly progressive mentality of the Council and its desire to return to the biblical sources, yet the whole discussion still remained inchoative. Yet the discussion did anticipate some of the ideas of the second session, and the question will be dealt with in that connection later.

Despite the many climaxes that followed, it became increasingly evident that a certain fatigue was spreading over the Council. In my opinion, this was ultimately due to the fact that everyone felt clearly that, in the voting of November 20 and the discussions on the liturgy, the Council had done its work for the time being. Further, the fathers seemed to feel that, for all practical purposes, what was needed now was new preparation. This work would have to be done in a completely new spirit differing from the spirit of the

THEOLOGICAL HIGHLIGHTS OF VATICAN II

earlier proposals, and the model for this reworking would have to be the spirit and language of the liturgy schema. The earlier preparatory work had been done in the defensive, anti-Modernistic tradition of the curia, most of whose offices had come into being during the battles of the last hundred years. The Council's decision meant nothing less than a basic overhauling of the view manifested in the preparatory work. It had initiated, in the concentrated effort and thought of the early weeks, a new beginning which now had to be carried forward. The job of working out details was not the business of the plenary assembly. What the *plenum* and only the *plenum* (the bishops from all over the world) could do had been done. They had reversed course and had given their orders.

Job of Bishops vs Committees

We would like to make clear once more just what all this meant. The Council had asserted its own teaching authority. And now, against the curial congregations which serve the Holy See and its unifying function, the Council had caused to be heard the voice of the episcopate—no, the voice of the universal Church. For, with and in the bishops, the respective countries, the faithful and their needs and their concerns were represented. What the bishops said and did was far more than an expression of a particular theological school. It was rather the expression of another school which they had all attended, the school of their

Bishops importance

very office, the school of communion with their faithful and with the world in which they lived.

There is much talk today in theological circles of the Church's "sense of faith" as a source of dogma. Such a source is not always fully trustworthy. Who can really determine what this "sense of faith" is? Here, however, the consciousness of faith of the whole Church had become genuinely concretized and energetically effective—so much so that, without denying the value of the three-year work of preparation, the Council had nevertheless unmasked it as largely inadequate and had demanded that the preparation be done all over again on a new basis. And so it was clear that a rather long adjournment was needed so that the texts which had to be so thoroughly revised might be presented again to the Council in a manageable form.

It is striking that the debate on the liturgy schema lasted longest, even though there was a basic agreement on this schema. But at second glance this was only natural. Precisely because the fathers were in basic agreement on the text as a whole, it made sense to argue over details. But in the case of the other texts, especially the revelation schema, the fathers ultimately could do no more than explain their discontent. It would be rather useless to discuss details of a text, the whole of which the Council was unwilling to accept in its proposed form.

Why more time on Liturgy?

52

THEOLOGICAL HIGHLIGHTS OF VATICAN II

The long adjournment of nine months was also welcomed on another count. Only thus could a second session be guaranteed a full assembly. It would have been impossible for the bishops from overseas, and especially those from South America and the mission countries, to make the long trip to Rome more than once a year. And if there had been a certain skepticism in the beginning about such a mammoth gathering, subsequent facts had shown its indispensability. Only it had been able to achieve that "horizontal" Catholicity that was one of the most precious fruits of the first session. Only it had been able to create that rich spiritual stimulation which in the end inspired and rejuvenated everyone present. The Council had turned out to be an intensive theological education for the bishops. Many who in the isolation of their ministry had been fully absorbed by their daily cares and labors had found a bridge to the intellectual life of the modern world and to all the great things that had awakened within the Church. They felt grateful for the gift they had been given. They, too, through the spirit of simplicity and service they had infused into the Council, had imperceptibly also enriched others.

The interval between the sessions had a twofold function given it in the final instruction of the pope. In this, Pope John simply formulated what the Council discussion had evolved. The tasks were:

1. To reformulate the schemata in line with the spirit of the Council majority.

2. To choose from the 70 schemata (now grouped under 20 headings) the most essential texts, to collate related texts and to condense the material in a form manageable for the Council. The commissions were not supposed to work out a handbook for specialists.

Clearly then, in view of the immense scope of the assignment, the interim period (which might seem rather long to the outsider) was in reality quite short. It appeared even dubious whether the work could be done in time. On the other hand, the Council had so often done the impossible that it was natural enough to become affected by Pope John's really contagious optimism and to take new hope.

Some may have been discontent because no text emerged from the session, nor any really palpable result. Yet the response to this should be clear from all that has been previously said, for it was precisely in this apparently negative outcome that the greatness, the surprise and the truly positive effect of the first session lie. For it was in this negative outcome that the spirit of the preparatory work was completely reversed. Here lay the truly epochal character of the first session.

PART TWO

The Second Session

I

PRELIMINARY NOTES

The death of John XXIII—this pope so great in his human humbleness—constituted a major turning point for the Council. This gentle pope had convoked the Council and imprinted on it his own features—liberty, optimism born of faith and willingness to be guided by the divine appeals which are heard by those who will listen. The question after his death was whether the Council would be continued at all. Part of the Italian press, for example, took for granted its indefinite adjournment. In this it no doubt echoed the desires of various segments of the Italian episcopate. The election of the Milanese archbishop Montini who had been on friendly terms with Pope John quickly lifted this uncertainty. But this election did not merely signify a continuation; it also marked a new beginning. This new beginning was expressed in several speeches and decisions of the pope to which brief reference must be made if an accurate account of the climate of opinion that influenced and permeated the Council during its second session is to be conveyed.

1. The Pope and Curial Reform

First must be mentioned an address which Pope Paul VI gave on September 21, 1963, on the occasion of a reception for members of the curia, and which dealt with the curia's significance and reform. To appreciate the importance of this address for the work of the Council, it must be recalled that the opposition between the Roman curia and the world episcopate did not appear for the first time at this Council; this opposition had marked the debates of the Council of Trent as well as those of the late Middle Ages. It may be said without exaggeration that this speech constituted not merely an episode in the history of curia and papacy but that it was also part of conciliar history. The speech took its cue from the debates of the first session and it outlined the possibilities and limits of the second session. But it should be noted that in this speech Pope Paul took a much more differentiated position than was generally revealed in the news reports. Without going into specifics, the following may indicate briefly its fundamental viewpoint.

The pope here invited the Council to deal with the question of curial reform and to consider, moreover, the creation of a new organ, a kind of episcopal council. This council was obviously not to be understood as subordinate to the curia but rather as a direct representation of the world episcopate. We shall deal with this question in greater detail in the course of our comments. The theme of curial reform was thus in a sense officially declared open for Council debate. The historical significance of this move can be properly appreciated only when one reflects that, in the debates of previous Councils, popes had also been willing to accept the possibility of curial reform. On those occasions, however, they had considered such reform as falling exclusively within their own competency. They regarded the curia as their personal affair on which a Council had no right to encroach. Admittedly, behind this loomed the fear of conciliarism—the point of view that sought to put the Council not merely above the curia but also above the pope himself. The pope's power to veto conciliar encroachments upon the curia ultimately helped safeguard the special position of the papacy, a position which had not yet been clarified theologically. The clarification of 1870 now shows its positive aspects. The pope was now in a position to extend without fear an invitation to the Council on an issue where his predecessors had always adopted a defensive attitude. Moreover, what was happening was that the traditional solidarity between pope and curia was now giving way to an unprecedented new solidarity between pope and Council.

Thus we can confidently say that the papal address on the curia represented a new and significant historical step. Yet it did not really mean a break with the past, for the Council had been asked to make proposals in this matter but not to make decisions. Thus the final decision remained with the pope. If this fact is kept in mind, the decentralization measures ordered by the pope at various later stages may be more accurately appraised. These measures resulted from the same combination of a daring step into the future with the preservation of the past which we found in Paul's address of September 21. Indeed, one can affirm that this is generally characteristic of Pope Paul's position vis-à-vis the Council. Everything he did afterward bore this same imprint: a willingness to welcome change and innovation, but always in keeping with the continuity of history. Despite all the differences in temperament between the two popes, this attitude is very like that of John XXIII who is supposed to have said of himself that he was the pope of those who step on the gas as well as those who step on the brake.

2. Revision of the Council's Statutes

A second event possessed equal significance for the continuation of the Council. The Council fathers (and their theologians) had become accustomed to the avalanche of papers and documents of all kinds that almost suffocated them during their stay in Rome. Among the papers they received shortly after their arrival was a modest brochure that contained a revision of the statutes of the Council. It included some major changes in the procedures that had been followed during the first session. Hubert Jedin, the historian from Bonn, had in 1960 addressed himself in an important article to this question of Council statutes. He had pointed out that, although statutes may seem mere technical instruments to facilitate the conduct of affairs, they have in reality great theological significance. For statutes control not only the practical functioning of the Council but also the way in which various forces are marshaled. Thus statutes have a way of predetermining decisions. So statutes can mirror and predefine the entire theology of a council. And the resultant theology is particularly effective because it is a realistic theology which practically predetermines the extent to which various forces influence a Council.

Jedin's analysis also makes clear that the history of the Church and its Councils is reflected in the history of Council statutes. This history shows a constantly increasing curialization. The statutes of the present Council had continued this trend. Indeed, the trend may have here reached a new climax, since the Council's working agencies, the commissions, were in structure closely linked with the corresponding curial congregations whose presidents and secretaries occupied in almost all cases similar positions on the Council commissions. They were thus able to wield power and take advantage of the opportunities inherent in these positions. Especially during the second session, this led to a very real dilemma. The commissions, which should have been the Council's own organs, coincided in leadership and technical staff with those of the autonomous curia. Therefore, tensions frequently developed between the desires of these commissions and the views of the Council majority. In any case the commissions were far from being what they were supposed to be—the mere executive agencies of the Council. Also historically important is that in both Vatican Councils the right to propose items for Council discussions had become the exclusive prerogative of the pope.

In view of this previous history, its background and implications, revised statutes were likely to evoke lively curiosity. Any changes were bound to be of inestimable significance for the theology and functioning of subsequent sessions. As it turned out the new text was not revolutionary. On the whole it left previous practice untouched. It would probably have been a mistake to try to completely rebuild a ship in mid-ocean. Nonetheless, the new text contained a number

62

of changes that, taken as a whole, indicated a distinct new direction. I will discuss only those factors now generally known so as to point up their basic meaning.

Most striking was the creation of a new governing body, consisting of four moderators. The presidium had been too large, too heterogeneous, and its members generally too old to provide real inspiration and leadership. The group of moderators was now expected to provide effective direction and also to give the Council a particular theological identity. The choice of persons was itself significant. At least Cardinals Lercaro, Suenens and Döpfner had unequivocally declared their theological views during the first session. By nominating them, the pope himself had pre-set the Council's theological mold. In their choice he had also shown his own attitude, an attitude confirmed by repeated expressions of sympathy for the cardinal from Belgium.

The second change we should mention is the strengthening of the commissions vis-à-vis their presidents. Although the incumbent presidents remained and with them the curial leadership, the sweeping powers they had possessed in the previous session were now to some extent curtailed. The rights of commission members, even those of minority groups, were now strengthened by a number of safeguards. But as was already suggested, these changes turned out in the course of this second session to be inadequate to bring about harmonious cooperation between the Council and its commissions. As a result, various regional episcopates proposed that commission presidents be changed so as to clearly separate the Council's organs from the curia. The pope finally resolved this by a somewhat unexpected compromise. The presidents remained but they were to be assisted henceforth by a second vice president and a second secretary. Furthermore, the number of commission members was increased partly through election and partly by papal appointment. Future developments would show how well this arrangement worked.

Thirdly, we must mention that the right to submit items for discussion was restored to the Council *plenum* (plenary assembly). Any suggestions endorsed by a minimum of 50 bishops could be channeled to the Council through the commission for extraordinary affairs. Thus initiative was no longer only a papal prerogative; it was now also a prerogative of the bishops.

Public opinion has been understandably very interested in a fourth point. Lay people were henceforth accepted as auditors. The way was thus opened for lay people to address the plenary assembly. Like theological experts, these lay people could also be consulted by the commissions. Here, too, an important historical step was taken, though still somewhat hesitantly.

THEOLOGICAL HIGHLIGHTS OF VATICAN II

Though the layman was merely granted the title of auditor, there was from this point on a real opportunity for him to take part as a responsible advisor in the work of the Council. Despite this and other improvements, the Council organization remained cumbersome, thus leading to criticism from within and from without, to discontent and even the suspicion that "the other side" was procrastinating, and so on. Looking back objectively, we must bear in mind that it is difficult for an assembly of 2,500 men, each accustomed to having the last word, to get used to working together. Nor should we forget that parties, and hence party alliances, were no part of the Council's structure. Indeed, such groupings would really have been wrong in view of the members' special responsibility to truth and the need for each to speak only for himself and his conscience. Yet without such groupings the formation of majority opinions is extraordinarily difficult.

I feel that, despite all justifiable criticism, we must not overlook the fact that the solution of such problems requires a certain amount of time. After all, a Council faces tougher problems than determining traffic controls or grain prices. Here spiritual changes were underway that needed time to mature. As in the previous session, it was precisely this common effort—which seemed so tedious to outsiders—that was so indispensable and central to the Council. Here is where spiritual encounters really developed, where people matured together through mutual influence. Here was enacted an episode in the Church's spiritual drama. Surely the regulations could have simply permitted the filing of written intentions with the commissions; the speeches in full assembly could thus have been dispensed with. But even though there was *de jure* no difference between the written and spoken word, nobody could deny that *de facto* they were different, for the spoken word resulted in the creation of new communities of thought and thus led to a new step forward. There was a constant give and take and the fathers listened as well as spoke. This procedural inefficiency left the spiritual event untouched. The Church progressed in unity, and for such progress no timetable can be prescribed—not even 1966. In any case a certain amount of patience is always requisite in coping with events of such profundity.

3. The Pope's Opening Address

On September 29, St. Peter's Basilica received within its walls the reconvened Council. As with Pope John XXIII the previous year, the pope's opening speech was a major event which set the program for the ensuing weeks and was often echoed in the speeches of the Council fathers. You had to hear it to fully appreciate how movingly it integrated theological considerations with personal spiritual testimony. The accents can, of course, be variously placed. What most impressed me was how _Christ-centered_ it was. The words of the liturgy, *Te, Christe, solum novimus* ("Only you, Christ, do we know"), were especially stressed. Reference to Christ as the *only* mediator, as the hope that guides our vision and our work, carried strong conviction. And the pope movingly evoked the painting in the apse of St. Paul Outside-the-Walls. In this mosaic, Christ the Pantocrator stands upright, and prostrate before him is Pope Honorius III, "small and insignificant, throwing himself down to kiss the feet of Christ, who infinitely surpasses him in greatness. This scene," the pope went on to say, "repeats itself here, we believe, not in the manner of artistic representation, but, in reality, here in our gathering." The ancient mosaic, reflecting as it does early Christian awareness of _Christ's primacy_, interpreted the present age and, as the pope saw it, served as a yardstick by which to measure events. All human greatness was dwarfed before the vision of the Lord. The pope's address ended on a note that again evoked this theme. *Christus praesideat*, the pope exclaimed: "May he, the Lord himself, be the real president of this Council."

PRELIMINARY NOTES

Also moving, though in a different way, was Pope Paul's cordial dialogue with his predecessor, Pope John XXIII. Addressing himself fraternally and respectfully to Pope John, Paul faithfully acknowledged the legacy the humble John had left to the Church. And Paul resolutely affirmed the greatness and binding force of this heritage. This affirmation, in view of the hesitancy and criticism of those who were anxious, could certainly not be taken as a matter of course. The saying goes that there is no one more dead than a dead pope. But this certainly did not apply here. It could almost be said that nobody was more alive at this Council than the dead pope. Possibly the Council fathers were even more impressed now by Pope John's humble acceptance of the divine will than they had been during his lifetime.

Finally, Pope Paul formulated a clearly outlined four-point program for the reconvened Council, a program that closely reflected the thoughts of his predecessor. The first task of the Council was to deal with the Church's interpretation of its own nature. The pope, without limiting free Council debate in the matter, here projected a kind of sketch of such a statement about the Church's nature. He saw the coming of the Spirit to Christ's disciples at Pentecost as an antetype of the Church. Thus the christological and Holy Spirit-centered elements were given preeminence by Paul in the definition of the

THEOLOGICAL HIGHLIGHTS OF VATICAN II

Church. The Church was seen as represented by the apostles as well as Peter, thus anticipating not only papal primacy but also the college of bishops. By designating the bishops as heirs of the apostolic college, the pope also anticipated a question which in the coming weeks would lead to much controversy. Paralleling the pope's invocation of the pentecostal coming of the Spirit (at the beginning of the address) was the concluding appeal to the communion of saints. He thus widened the horizon to include the heavenly Church, with which the praying Church sees itself as in permanent union. He also widened the horizon by his references to the separated Christian brethren and to mankind as a whole. We may here mention briefly the other tasks set by the pope. The second of these was the renewal of the Church, the third the reestablishment of unity among Christians, and the fourth the Church's dialogue with contemporary man. We need not here discuss these points in detail.

One more basic characteristic of the pope's speech must be mentioned here: its genuinely ecumenical tone. Apart from all details of the address, we can see this tone in the fact that its thought was not a product of any particular theological school, but derived directly from the original and common sources of Christianity, in which all are united together. The prayer for forgiveness, which was the heart of the ecumenical part of the address, may seem a little dry as we read it.

ecumenical

But those who heard it hardly could fail to be moved by it. They were able to feel the immense magnitude and newness of the moment and to sense that it was no ordinary prayer or something antecedently taken for granted. Now that we are used to this attitude, we take it in stride. Also, it was striking as the pope's personal testimony. Perhaps to us the pope's Roman rhetoric may sometimes seem a bit strange, but in this moment it touched our hearts. It was obviously no empty statement when he said: "Our voice is trembling and our heart is moved, because your presence [the observers'] is an unspeakable consolation to us and a source of joyous hope." This was a compelling moment, a moment of genuine emotion; the pope had turned to the separated brethren and sincerely expressed his desire to find ways to overcome the divisiveness of history, in which the burden of guilt is carried by both sides, and which can be bridged only in the spirit of love. This love must abandon all petty calculation and must look ahead to the Lord and not backward to selfish interests. The concluding words, spoken in Greek and Russian, seemed to me of great significance, in that here the framework of Latin had unmistakably been discarded. A Church which spoke in all languages had affirmed its hope for the unity of Pentecost.

II

WORK BEGINS: THE DEBATE ON THE CHURCH

All that has been said so far is only by way of introduction to the second session proper. Yet our efforts to clarify the pope's position have already given us an idea of the session's possibilities. As we turn now to the actual work of the session, we will see what roads the bishops traveled during the often dramatic weeks that followed. We recall that the workload that faced them when they first met in the fall of 1962 seemed overwhelming. In the nine months since the end of the first session an effort had been made to reduce this material to manageable proportions. The original 70 schemata were now reduced to 16 texts and their scope diminished. Plans at this point called for a 17th text, dealing with the Church's presence in the modern world and the burning issues of the times. The purpose was to provide directives from the viewpoint of faith, an unquestionably important problem if a thorny one.

However, even this reduced workload proved too sizeable. A more drastic pruning was inevitable, as subsequent events were to show. The final texts would, as it turned out, fit into a much smaller compass.

1. The New Draft of the Schema on the Church

The schema on the Church was first on the agenda for this session. We may here indicate briefly what its structure was at this point. In the form in which it emerged at the end of the adjournment (January to August, 1963), it contained five chapters, dealing successively with the mystery of the Church, the Church as the People of God (attempting, in close conjunction with the first, a description of the nature of the Church), the hierarchical structure of the Church, the laity, and the holiness of the Church. Other chapters were added in the course of the Council, as we shall see.

To understand the text newly submitted to the fathers, it may be useful to realize that it was mainly the work of Belgian theologians who belonged to Cardinal Suenens' circle. It reflected their position, midway between Roman and Spanish scholasticism, and the boldly modern writings of German and French theologians. Like any man-made text, it was not free of weaknesses and it left room for criticism, particularly in view of the fact that a Council document is supposed to be for all future time part of the essential record of the Church. Despite all this, there is no denying (as a perfectionist might deny) that the text was, in the main, a solid piece of work which provided a sound starting point for future discussion. In comparison with the 1962 text, it was obviously the kind of "leap forward" that Pope John XXIII had asked for. Later interpreters will always have to remember the several stages through which this text passed and, indeed, the very history of the concept of the Church. Only thus will they be able to understand the historical framework of the Council within which the Church was discussed.

What did the new draft text on the Church say? In which direction was it further developed through discussion during the fall of 1963? We can attempt answers by referring briefly to some of the draft's major elements. Chapters 1 and 2 deal with the mystery of the Church, as we have noted above. We should recall that this issue had for centuries been troublesome, more so than other questions. The definition of the Church, born in the battles of the Reformation, which had prevailed until the present century was that of Robert Bellarmine. It got off to a bad start by being a definition "against" something. Bellarmine, in opposition to the reformers' idea of an invisible Church, placed great stress on its institutional character. So

73

much did he emphasize the Church's juridical aspects that he was able to put this in the formula that the Church was as visible as the Republic of Venice. Pope Pius XII's encyclical on the mystical body (1943) had made a great step forward from that earlier position, but its still too-pointed idea of the Church's visibility made it all but impossible to give any status to Christians separated from Rome. Moreover, its too one-sided derivation of the Church's nature from the idea of Christ's mystical body had in some ways supported a one-sided view which, especially in Germany, had led to the notion of the Church as the ongoing life of Christ. This view easily led to a false identification of the Church with Christ. But even discounting this danger, the encyclical was one-sided in its viewpoint, however understandable this was in view of the historical circumstances surrounding its issuance.

By contrast, the new text returned wholeheartedly to the total biblical testimony about the Church. Here the idea of the "body of Christ" is complemented with that of the "People of God." Here the Church is seen as determined by pneumatological as well as christological elements; the Church is charismatic as well as sacramental in structure. In short, the idea of the Church evidences the full biblical polarity. Greater differentiation was now possible in discussing the question of membership in the Church, and a new ecumenical perspective was opened up. We shall discuss this later in more detail. From the outset, the question which excited theologians as well as Christians in general was the question of what accents the Council would set in its discussion, and in what direction it would develop the text. It is practically impossible to summarize the full answer of the Council, even in this session, because of the unlimited range of opinions. All theological schools of thought, from the extreme "right" to the extreme "left" (to borrow a misleading image from politics), came out into the open. Without distortion, however, we can point to two distinct leitmotivs.

2. The Church and History

The first of these two themes is the tendency to see the Church less statically and more in terms of the dynamism of its history, the history of salvation, as modern theology calls it. What was involved here was the realization that the Church is not a rounded-off and finished reality, defined once and for all and thus something beyond time and space. Rather, in its real essence the Church remains a Church on the way and represents in itself the history of God's dealing with mankind: the God who since the days of Adam and Abel has been seeking man out and has been traveling through history with him in the accomplishment of his covenant. Such was the living view of the Church that the Council sought to present: a Church which was incomplete and continually journeying with and toward the God who constantly called out to it. Such an understanding of the Church—as the continuing history of God's relationship with man—led naturally to what is called the "eschatological" view of the Church (see chapter 7 of the final text on the Church). For a view of the Church as continually in pilgrimage implies that the Church cannot be exclusively oriented toward the past, even though the Church does possess in the unique Christ-event its changeless and enduring center. But the Church must also bear in mind that this very Christ, to whom it looks back and from whom it proceeded, is also the Lord who comes. It is with its eyes on him that the Church marches into the future. A Christ-centered Church is thus oriented not merely toward past salvific events; it will always also be a Church moving forward under the sign of hope. Its decisive future and its transformation are still ahead. It must therefore always be open to what comes and always ready to shed fixed formulations with which it was once at home so as to march on toward the Lord who is calling and waiting.

So seen, the Church's image assumes a more human aspect. It is no longer necessary to see it as a sacrosanct entity which must artificially be protected from all criticism and reproach. If the Church means the journey of mankind together with its God, if it is essentially incomplete and always short of its goal, then it is still the sinful Church continually in need of renovation. It must always throw off its earthly bonds and whatever leads to feelings of self-satisfaction. As it turned out, this is what Council debate during this session increasingly emphasized: namely, that the Church, as the People of God on pilgrimage, is also always the Church under the sign of weakness and sin. It is a Church in continual need of God's forgiving kindness.

Finally, we may mention in this connection that it was especially the Latin countries that developed the idea that the Church is "the Church of the poor." This assertion undoubtedly lends itself to many interpretations and many misinterpretations. A certain sentimentality could lead to a kind of romanticizing of poverty, which is harmful to nobody so much as the poor themselves. But the idea is essentially sound and may be seen as the expression of an important spiritual reawakening. The Church has for a long time looked like a Church of baroque princes. It is now returning to the spirit of simplicity which marked its origins— when the "servant of God" chose to be a carpenter's son on earth and chose fishermen as his first messengers. If in the past (or even the present) the Church seemed too closely identified with the ruling classes, the term "Church of the poor" unquestionably expresses a project of fundamental importance, a willingness to break free of such chains. It also means that in the footsteps of Christ the Church is sent especially to the forgotten and the outcasts.

3. The Church as a Sign

Another aspect was the emphasis on the Church's sacramental character. "Sacramental" is used here in opposition to that superficial view which often enough tried to see the Church as established on the level of worldly legitimacy and to seek for the Church a place among worldly institutions. So, to demand that the Church acquire greater sacramental self-awareness was tantamount to a demand that it again consider and actualize itself as a sign. In St. Augustine's definition, *sacramentum* is the equivalent of *sacrum signum*—i.e., a holy sign. A Church that sees itself sacramentally understands that it partakes of the meaning of a sign, whose responsibility it is to point beyond itself. If the Church is a "sacrament," a sign of God's presence among men, then it does not exist for its own sake. Its responsibility becomes a responsibility of pointing beyond itself. It is like a window which best fulfills its function by allowing one to see greater things through it. At the same time, a sacramental understanding of the Church provides a theological starting point for a proper assessment of ecclesiastical office, i.e., of the hierarchy. This will ensure that an ecclesiastical office be seen not as a secular office but as a ministry in service of God's holy signs. This seems to be a deeper and spiritually more adequate concept.

4. Episcopal Collegiality

After these comments on the first two chapters of the 1963 text on the Church, we can turn to the third chapter and its problem—the structure of ecclesiastical office. Debate on this dramatically climaxed the second session, and understandably so. As long as discussion centered on theoretical questions about the nature of the Church, escape into non-committal statements was always possible. But questions of office stumbled up against hard facts. The facts served as touchstones, testing how far theory might be applied in everyday reality.

We should first recall that in the Church there are three sacramental hierarchical offices—deacon, priest and bishop. Despite some interventions in favor of a

WORK BEGINS: THE DEBATE ON THE CHURCH

deeper understanding of the office of priest, this gained little attention during this session's debate. Debate centered on the offices of deacon and bishop. We can begin with the office of bishop.

The main point of contention was the question of "collegiality." Speakers asked again and again that episcopal collegiality become once more a determining element in the Church's structure. What did they mean by this? The starting point of the whole line of thought was the fact that Christ selected 12 apostles—i.e., he used a number whose meaning was very precise. The number 12 immediately reminded Israelites of the 12 sons of Jacob, from whom the 12 tribes of Israel had sprung. At the time of Christ, Israel's tribal structure had long since disappeared, but it continued to live on in Israel's faith and hope. The reestablishment of all the tribes of God's people was expected at the time of salvation at the end of the world.

When Jesus called 12 men to be his immediate followers, his gesture was intelligible to everyone. It meant that now the end had arrived; these 12 represented the reestablished, final Israel. Another conclusion followed. The 12 men we customarily call "apostles"—i.e., messengers—did not get this general designation until after Pentecost when they began to be messengers of the Gospel Jesus entrusted to them. During Jesus' lifetime, they were primarily known as "the 12." Their first function was to symbolize by the number the fulfillment of Israel's hope which the Lord meant to accomplish. Thus none of the 12 had significance by himself, but only when united with the 11 others, because only with them was he part of the intended symbolic gesture. No one of the 12 stands isolated. Intrinsically they belong together. Together one might say they form a kind of "college."

The Council debate combined these insights with the well-known theological tenet that the bishops are successors of the apostles in order to shed new light on this idea. For if the apostles belonged together collegially, then it followed that their succession could not consist in individual bishops' following in the footsteps of the individual apostles. Rather, the apostolic community continued in the Church through the community of bishops. The college of bishops was the post-apostolic continuation of the college of the 12. But then, wasn't it valid to assume that no individual bishop possessed a significance of his own, but had his episcopal office precisely in his union with the others, who together continued the college of apostles. In other words, the bishops are essentially a college; the episcopal office is a collegial office; essential here is that the office of the individual bishop be correlated with the office of his fellow bishops. Bishops continue the community of the 12 only insofar as they are a college. They possess from this the power to govern in the Church of God.

The efforts of the Council were aimed at a new and clear-cut validation of this structure of ecclesiastical office. It is true that the Council in no way diminished the special position Peter occupied among the 12, in keeping with the special mission entrusted to him by the Lord, independently of collegiality. But the debate also brought out the fact that Peter remained one of the 12, and that he remained within the community and not outside of it. So no one even indirectly questioned the pope's special position as successor of St. Peter, as defined at Vatican Council I in 1870. But it was now possible to point more clearly to its inner context. Just as Peter belonged to the community of the 12, so the pope belongs to the college of bishops, regardless of the special role he fills, not outside but within the college.

It was easy to see that these rather theoretical considerations could trigger an important process of renewal, for this line of thought returned to the original spiritual structure of the Church, pushing aside all external and secular patterns of thought. Since the Middle Ages, a concept of the Church largely taken from politics had prevailed. This, for instance, led Bellarmine to draw his argument for the pope's primacy from Aristotle rather than from sacred scripture. To prove that monarchy was the best form of government was enough to prove the pope's right to primacy. In contrast to these and other such political and superficial notions which compared the Church with monarchy or other political models, the Council saw the Church once again as built up from those who partake of the body and the Word of the Lord. This conception focused once again on the community of bishops in communion with one another. This community in turn represents the community of the various Churches in communion with one another, from which the Church of God is built up. This view provided a bridge to the Eastern Churches which have kept alive a stronger consciousness of community than the West. It also emphasized that the individual bishop existed not for his own community alone, but that he shared in the overall responsibility for the Church; mutual responsibility was in fact the task of the entire Church. So viewed, Catholicity no longer meant merely looking toward Rome; it also meant looking toward one's neighbors. This "horizontal" element included orientation toward the neighbor and the joint assuming of Christian responsibility. Finally, such thoughts must lead to a search for practical ways of realizing collegiality—i.e., to the question of the bishops' common ministry. An outline of this was attempted in this session's debate of the draft schema on bishops and the governance of dioceses.

Collegiality is Practical

As mentioned earlier, no subject was so controversial during this session as the question of collegiality because of its important practical consequences. The forces which had up to now directed the operations of the universal Church understandably thought of collegiality as the forsaking of tried and true traditions in favor of vague and very dangerous visions of the future. Moreover, they considered the theological basis of these visions questionable. Yet their recalcitrance did not prevent an eventual positive decision. In the famous test vote of October 30, the majority of the fathers answered positively the related questions of the moderators. Though the vote itself was afterward much criticized, its value as a poll of opinion remained undiminished. We shall show in detail at the end of this section that the way the pope confirmed the Council's decrees at the close of the session implied his clear-cut preference for collegiality.

5. The Deacons

We may now turn briefly to that other important feature of the Church's official structure—the diaconate. In contrast to Eastern Church practice, the Latin Church has long considered the office of deacon a way station on the road to the priesthood. The draft text proposed restoration of the independent diaconate. The movement supporting this change was widespread, and it mainly came from Latin America and many mission countries, particularly in Southeast Asia. African spokesmen seemed more reserved on this issue. A look at the way Latin American bishops argued their position will help us understand the problem.

There may be enough priests in Latin America to baptize, and perhaps even marry and bury, the people in their region, but they are insufficient to promulgate the Word of God in the vast reaches of their subcontinent. All they can handle is a superficial sacramentalization. They cannot do an even halfway adequate job of preaching the Gospel; yet without this there can be no real Christian penetration. This suggested the similar situation in the early Church, when the apostles were threatened, due to the external demands of their pastorate, with loss of freedom to preach the Word. Their solution was to create the office of "the Seven," which became the model for the diaconate in the Church (Acts 6, 1-6). Was this not the answer to the problem? Such retrospective reflections showed that the institutionalized framework of the Church permitted a much more flexible reaction to the varying needs of the age than had been assumed in the past. From its very origin, the office of deacon had been a dynamic way of reacting to new challenges. It offered the same opportunity again and provided a framework comprehensive enough to allow considerable variations depending on the different needs of various ecclesiastical regions.

Taking all this into account, it is not difficult to see that the restoration of the diaconate was urged primarily on the basis of two important positive considerations. In the first place it reflected a real hunger for the Word of God. To proclaim it effectively, new ways had to be sought out. People were awakened from the torpor of a Christianity of mere sacramentalism, very little different from magic and not productive of the faith which comes from hearing. On the other hand, the idea of the restored diaconate reflected the desire to make the spiritual ministry once again flexible and dynamic. The creation of a ministry that did not require celibacy (without in any way affecting the celibacy of priests) meant a likely increase in vocations, which in many cases had been decreasing sharply in number.

Many a speech made in this connection will never be forgotten by those who heard it. Like a cry of distress, the words of Bishop Kemerer of Posadas, Argentina, echoed through the Council hall on October 14: "Venerable fathers! Do not destroy our hope. This schema opens the door to the restored diaconate. We do not oblige you to enter. But permit entrance to those who may wish it."

Latin American chapters

This may be the proper place to emphasize the intensity and liveliness which marked Latin American Catholicism at the Council. Obviously we will have to correct some widespread misconceptions. It was noteworthy that on the first day of the Council two Latin American bishops requested that the schema on the Blessed Virgin be incorporated in the text on the Church. They explained that a danger existed that their populations would regard Marian piety as a completely independent thing and that they would cease seeing Mary in relation to Christ. In general it may be said that the center of gravity of this second session was somewhat different from that of the first. Central Europe did not dominate the proceedings quite as much, and Latin America and the missionary countries very clearly moved into the limelight. In 1962 they seemed more or less dependent upon European initiatives. By now they had become independent collaborators in the work of renewal, from which they expected an answer to urgent needs in a situation both full of danger and full of hope.

6. The Layman

The discussion on ecclesiastical offices had already made the discussion of the Church far more concrete.

When the Council came to consider the schema on bishops and the governance of dioceses, the debate became even more concrete and thus sometimes even more dramatic. What was primarily involved here was simply the application of the principles evolved during the debate on collegiality, so that the debates held on November 5-8, 1963, are really part of the collegiality discussion which we saw above as the central effort of the second session. I will therefore move on to this at the cost of passing only briefly over two important chapters of the schema on the Church—those dealing with the call to holiness and with the position of the layman in the Church, a topic especially important now.

But here I would like to make just one remark. In the discussion of both chapters, theologically significant observations were made that are bound to affect the life of people in the Church in the long run. There was a really liberating progress made in dealing with holiness—an idea which hitherto had seemed to be confined within monastic walls. However, it cannot be denied that the debate on the laity remained somewhat colorless and tedious, and this despite the proliferation of statements about it. The only exceptions were the animated attack on the text by Cardinal Ruffini on October 16 and the great speech by Cardinal Suenens on October 22. The tedium was due perhaps to the fact that the questions were formulated in too general and noncommittal a fashion. The debate became concrete when Cardinal Suenens demanded that women be admitted as lay auditors and when he asked that along with the hierarchical structure of the Church there be recognized a charismatic structure based on the prophets as well as the apostles. The debate became more concrete in a different way when the cardinal from Palermo largely denied the existence of charisms in the post-apostolic Church and when he reduced the function of laymen for all practical purposes to obedience to the hierarchy. This antithesis indicates the scope of the debate. Yet the other speakers did not succeed in making it lively. It was especially striking that despite all efforts no one was able to provide a positive definition of the layman. This might have been the real reason for the feeling of dissatisfaction which no well-intentioned discussion could have dispelled.

It had been customary to see the layman as the antithesis of the priest and the religious—as the one who is neither one nor the other. This is an old habit. What is so peculiar is that a widespread modern version of lay theology maintains this double negative as a starting point—a layman is neither priest nor monk—and tries to present it as something positive. This is the basis on which lay piety and lay spirituality are defined. But salesmanship does not turn a negation into something positive. No wonder that a closer look reveals that no positive concept of the laity exists. No positive concept can be derived from a negative original definition, even if this is later acclaimed as something wonderful. If progress is to be made here, theologians have to stop deriving the positive view of the layman from non-ecclesiastical and secular factors and must stop explaining the layman's position within the Church negatively. The question to ask is whether there are positive *ecclesiastical* categories in the Church besides those of the priest and the monk. The 12th chapter of Paul's first epistle to the Corinthians, which loomed in the background of the speech by Cardinal Suenens, offers plenty of food for thought here, but very little use was made of it during this debate.

III

PRACTICAL QUESTIONS: BISHOPS' CONFERENCES, BISHOPS' COUNCIL AND CURIAL REFORM

We finally come to the discussion of the schema on the bishops. As mentioned before, the basic idea was to concretely implement the concept of collegiality. To go to the heart of the matter, this goal was to be accomplished in two complementary ways: decentralization and centralization. The decentralizing tendency sought to grant to the bishops as an ordinary part of their episcopal office a series of powers which had been concentrated up to now in the papacy. Through this decentralization a corresponding measure of independence could be developed in the various pastoral sectors of the Church without being unduly restricted by continual appeal to Rome. The increased powers of the bishops would be supplemented through the institutional development of bishops' conferences. These conferences would revive the synodal structure of the ancient Church. They would also integrate the power of the individual bishop into the framework of the collegial structure of his office and would facilitate the formation of various regional outlooks within the unity of the one Church.

This tendency toward regional autonomy should not discount the value of union—especially in an age when mankind is seeking unity: thus the idea of creating an episcopal council in Rome. Such a council was not supposed to be a subdivision or supercommittee within the curia, but rather be a counterpart to it. It was not supposed to be part of the papal bureaucracy but rather an organ of the world episcopate. It would be something like a Council extended into the Church's everyday life. This would offer an opportunity for the representatives of the universal episcopate to meet regularly at the center, to exchange experiences and, together with the pope, to jointly serve the universal Church. By announcing at the end of the session the establishment of such an episcopal council, the pope made an important decision in this matter. Without exaggerating the immediate effect of such a step, there is no denying that it has set into motion a promising renewal of the structure of the Church.

Closely related to all this was the debate about curial reform. There is no need to go into detail here about this; we have already discussed its basic aspects. I would like to briefly comment on the best known episode of this debate, the much discussed oratorical duel between Cardinals Frings and Ottaviani on November 8. Jean Daniélou has said that this was an institutional and not a theological battle. This is basically true. At stake here was not a theoretical problem but rather the concrete way in which the Holy Office (since changed) was supposed to function. However, the repercussions of this incident would not have been so extraordinary had it not had profound implications. One might perhaps be justified in saying that the speech of the cardinal from Cologne made a realistic contribution on the theme of Christian liberty, this is what gave the episode great theological importance. Frings recognized that there are perversions of liberty which destroy liberty. But he also stressed that liberty and the respect for individual rights must be recognized in the Church if faith is to flourish and live in our time.

The speech could also be considered significant in another aspect. It showed readiness to expose, as manmade and temporal, forms that had been considered sacrosanct, and to introduce the positive results of modern legal thinking into ecclesiastical structures. These structures had often taken shape during the age of absolutism and therefore were all too human in origin. To present a complete picture, it should be added that the personal relationship between the two cardinals became much more cordial as a result of this controversy; a remarkable example, which might be taken as an indication of the intellectual and spiritual climate prevailing at the Council.

IV

INTERLUDE: THE MARIOLOGICAL QUESTION

One last aspect of the debate on the Church must be mentioned: the question of Mariology. The theological commission had carried into the plenary session two different opinions on this matter. Cardinal König of Vienna explained the view of those who desired that there be no separate schema about Mary but that the text on the Mother of God be integrated into that on the Church. In this way the statement about Mary could be integrated into the total ecclesiological picture. Cardinal Santos of Manila expressed the opposing view of those who wanted a separate schema on Mary. As is well known, the vote that took place on October 29, five days after these speeches, resulted in a slight majority in favor of those who wanted the text on Mary integrated with that on the Church. As things finally worked out, the chapter on

Mary & Church

Mary was incorporated during the next session into the text on the Church. Thus a better understanding of the status of Mary was achieved. With Mariology integrated into ecclesiology, the idea of the Church now encompasses the heavenly Church with the result that the eschatological as well as the spiritual aspects of the Church are strengthened. It is now also much clearer that the nature of the Church is not tied up exclusively with the temporal dimensions nor fully defined in terms of visible institutions, but that it extends into the future, into an area beyond human intervention and disposition. Such an enlarged picture of the Church, which includes those who have consummated their earthly lives, also implies an acknowledgment of a liturgical norm. The liturgy sees itself as performed in community with the saints.

In the last analysis, wherever Christian liturgy is celebrated, the community of the faithful is encompassed in that cosmic liturgy where all the world and all the saints adore God. Finally, it seems to me that the inclusion of the figure of the Mother of God can also shed some light on the mystery of the Church. In her own life Mary appeared as the humble servant exalted in her humility by God. She exemplifies the paradox of grace that touches those who cannot accomplish anything by themselves. She personifies the Church of the poor, the Church that moves through history as a hum-

Church not institution

Mary

ble servant, and by that very fact is in a position to express the mystery of God's promise and proximity. Mary also embodies the Church that sprung from the root of Israel and that carries the hope of the world that secretly lives beneath its heart during the strenuous journey through history. Thus the decision in the matter of Mariology did open the way to something positive. It may have brought us nearer the time when it will again be conceivable that Christians of different denominations will understand one another on this particularly divisive issue.

V

THE QUESTION OF ECUMENISM

1. The Text and the Debate

We come now to the last text debated—the draft schema on ecumenism. At this stage there were three sections. One series of chapters dealt with ecumenical problems as such; one other chapter dealt with the relationship of the Church of Israel and another with the question of religious liberty. All these themes were clearly related to one another, yet they dealt with three distinct problems. As a matter of fact, three separate texts had been planned originally and only external circumstances had brought them together into one overall document. Eventually they would again appear separately. We will deal here with the three chapters on the ecumenical problem, the chapters which formed the basis for the eventual *Decree on Ecumenism*.

We might here be more tempted than in other questions to simply narrate the story of what happened, describing, for example, the great speeches made on this topic which ushered in a new era of intra-Christian relations. A breathless hush came over St. Peter's Basilica when Coadjutor Archbishop Elchinger (Strasbourg) in his intervention of November 19, 1963, admitted the Church's past errors: "Until now we have often not dared to confess historical facts which are less than favorable to the reputation of our Church. Now the time has come…to admit and confess historical truth—even when it is bitter….Until now, when there were controversies between separated Christians, we frequently rejected as completely false doctrines we thought erroneous. Now the time has come to recognize with greater respect that there is also a partial truth, in fact often a profound truth in every doctrine taught by our separated brethren, which we should profess along with them....Until now many Catholics, including clergy and hierarchy, have adhered in too passive and static a fashion to the truth of revelation in the Church....Now the time has come for all of us, each in our own way, to probe ever more deeply the divine truth in living faith....Until now, especially in the Latin Church of recent times, we have frequently confused uniformity—both in liturgical rites and in theological doctrines which express divine revelation—with unity in faith, love and Christian worship. Now the time has come...to recognize, honor and cultivate the liberty of the children of God in the Church of Christ, both freedom of individuals and of communities...." On the same day, Cardinal Léger of Montreal spoke against doctrinal "immobilism," opposing to this the saying of St. Augustine: "Seek that you may find, and find that you may continue to seek." He demanded of the Church the kind of intellectual humility that would not make an unqualified claim to possess the whole truth, an obstacle in the way of those seeking a deeper understanding of Christ's revelation.

Much else could be mentioned, including the speeches of the Maronite and Melchite rite bishops, which often highlighted Council discussion. A really comprehensive report would have to go into the two chapters later detached. First of these was the chapter on the Church and Israel, with its dark historical background so full of tears and blood, as well as Cardinal Bea's moving presentation of this text. We would have to discuss the politically-inspired opposition from Eastern Christians living in Islamic countries; these bishops demanded that the text on the Jews be counterbalanced by a declaration about Islam, a demand which was to be met in the final text on non-Christian religions. A comprehensive report would also have to discuss the text on religious liberty, an issue which also has a very dark past and which will be one of the most important items of the two following sessions. We should also have to mention the reaction of non-Catholic observers which at this point was often rather critical and cool. But this reaction at this stage indicated that the dialogue had entered a concrete and serious phase. The era of noncommittal good feeling had vanished now that direct contact had been made with decisive issues. Here growing criticism meant growing closeness.

But we cannot tell this whole story here. We must limit ourselves to analysis of the basic theological problem of the ecumenical debate—to asking how the text viewed the relation between "the Church and the Churches" and thus to how it saw the ecumenical problem as a whole. To clarify this, we must comment first on the relationship of the schema on ecumenism to that on the Church.

2. Comparison to the Schema on the Church

a. *The Basic Relationship between the Two Texts*

Like the schema on the bishops, so the schema on ecumenism was intended to concretize the meaning of the schema on the Church and to apply it practically. It therefore presupposed the text on the Church and depended upon it. This relationship of dependence was also expressed in the juridical terminology employed. The schema on the Church was planned as a "Constitution" and that on ecumenism as a "Decree." The latter was thus to be a kind of concrete application of theoretical principles. We must also bear in mind that the schema was not addressed to non-Catholics, nor was it intended to be some kind of unity manifesto. Rather, it was a pastoral directive to Catholics to turn their attention to ecumenism. Its intention was to promote ecumenism by preparing the Catholic Church for ecumenical thought and action.

Viewing the text as a pastoral application of the doctrine in the schema on the Church, the question arises as to what basis the Church text offers for such application. One might say first that the text on the Church was favorably predisposed toward ecumenical thinking in that its basic theological line was ecumenical. It was not directed against anyone; it sought to derive its thought from common origins and tried to keep in view the *totality* of tradition. It also attempted to slough off particularisms coming from Latin or scholastic sources and to keep the door open on all legitimate theological questions. Such a text would have been unthinkable without the prior existence of the ecumenical movement. It would be an exaggeration to say that it grew out of the ecumenical movement in the same way the *Constitution on the Sacred Liturgy* grew out of the liturgical movement. Nonetheless it was decisively influenced by it. This was evident in the attempt to define the nature of the Church. The title of the text no longer referred in scholastic fashion to the "nature of the Church" but spoke rather of its "mystery." Ecumenism also was to be found in the view of ecclesiastical offices as ministry, of laymen as within the framework of the unity of the holy People of God, and of holiness as a gift God continually gives to a Church in constant need of forgiveness. The enumeration could continue. It might be said that the text as a whole manifested not merely the Church's teaching authority, but also its capacity for listening.

b. *Positive Statements on Ecumenism in the Schema on the Church*

Explicit references to the ecumenical question occur only where the problem of Church membership arises. The drafting of the text went through three phases. A comparison between them points unmistakably to a steady development in the direction of openly ecumenical thinking.

(1) The *first schema* of 1962 still clung to the traditional scholastic formula which saw membership in the Church as dependent on the joint presence of three prerequisites: baptism, profession of the same faith and acceptance of the hierarchy headed by the bishop of Rome. Only those who met these three requirements could be called members of the Church. Obviously this was a very narrow formulation. Other formulations were not necessarily excluded, yet the result was that the notion of "member of the Church" could be applied only to Catholics. With such an answer to the question of Church membership, it became very difficult to describe the

Christian dignity of the non-Catholic Christian. His association with the Church was expressed only in the questionable concept of the *votum Ecclesiae*, meaning that non-Catholic Christians belonged to the Church by virtue of their "desire" to be a part of it. Since "Church" here obviously meant the Roman Catholic Church, it can easily be seen that such a description was insufficient. In the first place, it was based on a fictitious psychology since it ascribed to the separated brethren a "desire" they never (at least consciously) entertained. An equally weighty objection is that these Christians were in effect put on the same level as non-Christians, since the hidden desire to be a member of the Church was also ascribed to the latter. Finally, one could object that this whole approach suffered from a purely individualistic point of view. This point was made several times in the course of the general debate on this schema on the Church that took place in 1962. Accordingly, modifications were made in the text submitted in 1963 to the Council fathers.

(2) The new text avoided the expression "member of the Church," hallowed by long usage in Catholic theology. Use of this expression would have immediately aroused the scholastic theologians who saw this notion as

necessarily including the three above-mentioned prerequisites. In view of these difficulties, the decision was taken to avoid this controversial term. The new text describes the relationship between the Church and non-Catholic Christians without speaking of "membership." By shedding this terminological armor, the text acquired much wider scope. This made possible a much more positive presentation of the way Christians are related to the Church as well as a positive Christian status for Christians separated from Rome. The text submitted to the fathers in the fall of 1963 states therefore that multiple internal ties existed among Christians. Baptism was one such tie as was the name of Christian which baptism conferred. There was also common faith in Christ, Son of God and Savior; there was common possession of other sacraments, prayers and spiritual values, and, finally, an inner hidden unity in the Holy Spirit.

(3) The theological commission further amended the text in view of the Council discussion, with due regard for the objections presented by the non-Catholic observers. It retained the basic formulation but made a number of significant additions. It included as another bond of unity the common possession

of sacred scripture, aimed at Protestant Christianity. Furthermore the pneumatological aspect was reinforced. Speaking of union in the Holy Spirit, the text said that his sanctifying power also works in those Christians, and that Catholics, in turn, are in constant need of purification and renewal. Finally, and perhaps most important of all, the text observed that non-Catholic Christians recognized other sacraments besides baptism, and that they received them "in their own Churches and ecclesial communities." Thus allowance was made for a major misgiving on the part of the Protestant observers who saw their Churches as bypassed in the text or broken down into their individual components. They had therefore felt misunderstood, indeed snubbed. The new text now says unmistakably and clearly, although in passing, that these Christians exist not merely as *individuals* but as Christian communities which are given positive Christian status and ecclesial character.

c. *The Limitations of the Schema on the Church*

We face here the *principal criticism* non-Catholic observers made of the schema on the Church. As they saw it, the official text of 1963 spoke of non-Catholic

Protestants as individuals or Communities

Christians only as individuals, thus bypassing the real heart of the ecumenical problem. Before dealing with this question, we want to comment briefly on the methodological problem broached here. It is certainly true that it would have been possible and in many respects even desirable had the schema on the Church taken a clear-cut position on the ecumenical problem, rather than leave detailed treatment of this problem to the schema on ecumenism. It seems to me, however, that there are also real advantages in the omission, because now the Council's thought on the ecumenical question can be seen only by combining the two texts. The doctrinal text on the Church is clearly open to supplementation, and this is provided by the schema on ecumenism. By merely juxtaposing the two texts, the second developing a view only hinted at in the first, the Council in effect characterizes the first—the doctrinal text on the Church—as an open and far from comprehensive text. This factor has sometimes received inadequate attention.

The doctrinal text on the Church is no theological treatise or an all-encompassing theological description of the Church. It rather indicates a path to be followed. Since this text does not pretend to be a doctrinal manual, it does not intend to supply comprehensive and exhaustive information. It seems to me that we would basically misunderstand the meaning of any Council text were we to demand that it reflect all valid theological points of view. Therefore, the bishops were right in opposing on several occasions the "profundity" of their theologians who were all somewhat tempted to get their favorite ideas into the texts of the Council. The bishops were well advised to avert such theological perfectionism and to insist that the Council was not supposed to offer a complete ecclesiology. We might even say that the closer a text came to theological perfection, the more restricted and closed it would be thought in the future. History amply illustrates this. The greater the hurry to import the best theology of the moment into a Council's statements, the narrower such statements later seemed. So one can only say: Beware of theological perfection! It might not leave room enough for future development. In general, the texts of a Council are not meant to save work for theologians. Rather, they should stimulate such work and open new horizons. If necessary they should also mark off the boundaries between solid ground and quicksand.

The text on the Church was kept open primarily because it was to be supplemented by a text on ecumenism which would develop a viewpoint only hinted at in the Church text. Taking both texts into account, we can view in a positive light the undeniably limited ecumenical outlook of the schema on the Church. The combination of the texts points to the intrinsic incompleteness of the total statement on ecumenism.

3. Factual Aspects of the Problem

To get to the heart of the ecumenical problem, I will begin with the comments of Professor Edmund Schlink of Heidelberg to the press on October 23, 1963. Speaking in Rome, he presented his views on the status of the ecumenical problem as reflected in the texts of the Council. The debate on ecumenism had not as yet begun; the Council was still busy with the schema on the Church. Today Professor Schlink might formulate his position in a somewhat different way, but issues remain the same. It may therefore be in order to review Professor Schlink's questions, since our purpose here is simply to clarify those issues.

Professor Schlink started with the premise that the "Roman Church" (he preferred not to say "Roman Catholic") identified itself in an exclusive manner with the one, holy, catholic and apostolic Church. Whenever Rome recognized a bond between individual non-Catholic Christians and the Church, this implied that these Christians considered themselves united with the Roman Church. Schlink, however, insisted that these Christians saw themselves as receiving grace and salva-

from where does say flow?

tion as members of *their own* Churches and not as members of the Roman Church. Not only did the Catholic position misinterpret the self-awareness of non-Catholic Christians; it was also out of line with the New Testament. Finally, it followed with unavoidable logic from this position that non-Roman Christians were required to "leave their Churches and be incorporated into the Roman Church." These observations led Professor Schlink to ask: "What is the meaning then of Roman Catholic ecumenism? What is the meaning of the new way of addressing non-Roman Christians as 'separated brethren' instead of as 'heretics' and 'schismatics' as in the past? What is the meaning of the praise given to the 'spiritual fruits' to be found in non-Roman Churches, and what is meant by 'accepting the witness of their devotion…and their theological insights'? Is not all this an effort aimed at absorption? Is not this kind of ecumenism, as some Protestant Christians suspect, merely a continuation of the Counter-Reformation with other, more accommodating methods?"

To this Professor Schlink opposed a completely different concept of the ecumenical movement. Such a movement, in his view, should lead to community among the separated Churches and not to their absorption by one of the Churches. It is important to note that Professor Schlink deliberately formulated the latter part of his discussion in the form of questions and not of assertions. Therefore, these questions obviously constitute an invitation addressed to Catholic theologians to engage in discussion. In the same spirit of positive effort toward mutual understanding, I will try here to respond to this invitation.

It is difficult to answer both briefly and suitably. In any case the answer cannot pretend to be more than an attempt. A starting point is provided by Professor Schlink's view that the ecumenical movement is not supposed to be an effort of absorption of the separated Churches by one of the existing Churches (as in the view of the Catholic Church). This view evidently reflects the conviction that none of the "existing Churches" is *the* Church of Jesus Christ but rather that they are various concretizations of the one Church which does not exist as such. None therefore can claim to be *the* Church. It is certain, however, that a Catholic cannot share Schlink's conviction. Ever since the days of primitive Catholicism, which reaches back to the time of the New Testament, it has been considered essential to believe that *the* Church really exists, although with shortcomings, and that this has been reflected concretely in the visible Church which celebrates the liturgy. The Catholic is convinced that the visible existence of the Church is not merely an organizational cover for a real Church hidden behind it, but on the contrary that, for all its humanity and insuf-

The Catholic Church is The Church

ficiency, the visible Church is the actual dwelling place of God among men, that it is *the* Church itself. To that extent Professor Schlink's contention that there exists an identification of the Catholic Church with the Church of Jesus Christ is valid.

Catholic theology, too, recognizes a plurality of Churches. It has, however, a different meaning from the plurality of Professor Schlink. What Catholics mean is that a multiplicity of Churches exists within the framework of the *one* and visible Church of God, each of which represents the totality of the Church. In close communion with one another they help build up, within the framework of a unity born of a vigorous multiplicity, the one Church of God. There exists a Church of God in Athens, in Corinth, in Rome. It exists likewise in Trier, Mainz and Cologne. Each local community assembled with its bishop around the table of the Lord, listening to the Word of the Lord, partakes of the essence of the Church and may therefore be called a "Church." To be a Church, however, it must not exist in isolation but must be in communion with the other Churches which, together with it, make up the one Church.

This consideration permits the following additional comments:

(a) The New Testament recognizes a plurality of Churches only in the above-mentioned sense. By this plurality the New Testament (whose historical setting is admittedly quite different from ours) does *not* mean separated denominational communities, but rather the many worshiping communities which all are nonetheless one. This unity does not arise from some common aspiration, but rather from the concreteness of the joint sharing in the Word and body of Jesus Christ.

(b) Catholic theology has always accepted the possibility of the plurality of Churches. It should however immediately be added:

(c) This plurality of Churches has in fact increasingly receded in favor of a centralized system; in this process the local Church of Rome has, so to speak, absorbed all the other local Churches. In this way unity was curtailed in favor of uniformity. This state of affairs, which the Council has attempted to correct, was a cause for the separation among the Churches. Yet it also provided a positive ecumenical point of departure for the Catholic Church. The ecumenical movement grew out of a situation unknown to the New Testament and for which the New Testament can therefore offer no guidelines. The plurality of Churches, which should have had a legitimate existence within the Church, had receded increasingly into the background. This explains why this plurality, for which there was no room *within* the Church, was developed *outside* of it in the form of autonomous separate Churches. The Council's recognition of this is tantamount to its seeing that uniformity and unity are not identical. Above all, it means that a real multiplicity of Churches must be made alive again within the framework of Catholic unity.

These considerations may open the way to answer the question raised by Professor Schlink. Does Catholic ecumenism not ultimately amount to the absorption of the other Churches? Is it not therefore the Counter-Reformation in a different form? As long as unity was identified with uniformity, the Catholic goal could not help but appear to non-Catholic Christians as complete absorption into the present form of the Church. However, the recognition of a plurality of Churches within the Church implies two lines of change:

(a) The Catholic has to recognize that his own Church is not yet prepared to accept the phenomenon of multiplicity in unity, he must orient himself toward this reality. He must also recognize the need for a thorough Catholic renewal, something not to be accomplished in a day. This requires a process of opening up, which takes time. Meantime, the Catholic Church has no right to *absorb* the other Churches. The Church has not yet prepared for them a place of their own, but this they are legitimately entitled to.

(b) A basic unity—of Churches that remain Churches, yet become *one* Church—must replace the idea of conversion, even though conversion retains its meaningfulness for those in conscience motivated to seek it.

To remove all misunderstanding, I must add that the above idea still differs from the ecumenical movement as seen by Professor Schlink, despite all the areas of agreement. His notion of the ecumenical movement stems from a different view of the Churches' visibility and unity. As he sees it, all separated Churches are equally legitimate manifestations of the Church. None of them constitutes *the* Church. For Catholics, however, there is *the* Church, which they identify with the historic continuity of the Catholic Church. Therefore, the Catholic cannot demand that all the other Churches be disbanded and their members be individually incorporated into Catholicism. However, he can hope that the hour will come when "the Churches" that exist outside "the Church" will enter into its unity. But they must remain in existence as *Churches*, with only those modi-

Unity & plurality

(Churches w/in The church)

fications which such a unity necessarily requires. Accordingly, two observations can be made:

(a) It is true that the Catholic Church cannot simply adopt Professor Schlink's view, based on the idea that all existing Churches have practically equal rights. This is tantamount to asking that the Catholic Church convert to Protestantism, since this view corre sponds to the Protestant concept of the Church. This makes as little sense as the opposite.

(b) Although the Catholic Church considers itself as *the* Church of Christ, it nonetheless recognizes its historic deficiency. It recognizes the fact that the plurality of "Churches," which should exist *within* it, exists today outside it, and perhaps could only exist outside.

4. The Movement of the Council

Thus the last step has been taken. The New Testament recognizes the plurality of Churches only within the unity of the one Church and never in the form of separated denominational Churches. In view of the historical Christian situation, the Council tried to see the plurality of "Churches" outside the unity of the one Church. It conceded to non-Catholic Christian communities the honorable name of "Church." Though they are not "*the* Church," they are really "Churches." Such a formula should go a long way in meeting the self-awareness of these communities. This term "Churches" implies the Catholic Church's admission that it did not leave proper room for this multiplicity in its oneness. It thus is continuously challenged to open itself to a real ecumenical future. To be precise, we must see something more of the background.

As to the Orthodox Churches, their recognition as Churches has a long history. This is not true, however, of the Reform denominations. The Eastern Churches maintained their structure intact when the East and West broke off communion in the year 1054. Everything the Church considered necessary for a "Church" remained. Only the tie with the Western Churches was broken. This explains why the Roman Catholic Church has officially never ceased to apply the term "Church" to the Eastern Churches.

However, the Protestant break with Rome was of a different nature. It fundamentally challenged the concept of the Church and created a new form of the community: the *confession* or *denomination*. Word now is more important than sacrament and hierarchy. The new communities did not all consider themselves Churches. Nothing for instance could have been further from the thought of Luther than the creation of a Lutheran Church.

116

The situation has changed considerably since then. In many cases the confessions are vitally aware of themselves as Churches. Today, for example, the Lutheran tends to take for granted the existence of a Lutheran Church. This is, however, not always the case. Here was one of the difficulties the Council had to face; it had to recognize the divergence and difference in viewpoints without any glossing over of diversity. In line with Cardinal König's suggestion, the term "ecclesiastical communities" was introduced in the final text along with the term "Churches," thus leaving the necessary room for special structures and different points of view. The Roman Catholic Church made an important new doctrinal step in officially describing the Eastern Churches and the ecclesiastical communities of the Reformation as "Churches." Thus the Catholic Church acknowledged its historic guilt and insufficiency and admitted that the Christianity outside it could not be described adequately in negative concepts of heresy and schism. Here we find a sober practical approach, giving the greeting "brothers" a meaning that goes far beyond worthless sentimentality.

One other observation. No doubt the concrete significance of the *Decree on Ecumenism* (like the text on the Church) will largely depend on how successfully its spirit is translated into practical ecclesiastical life and the law that gives this life its forms and limits. A number of important suggestions on this have already been

THE QUESTION OF ECUMENISM

made, especially in regard to mixed marriages, and to common prayer and common testimony before the non-Christian world. Things here are still in a state of flux. Despite some excellent beginnings, much depends on the daily patience and goodness of Christian people. For that reason, appeal to the ecumenical spirit will in the final analysis remain decisive; without this spirit, ecumenical words must remain empty talk.

VI

THE ACHIEVEMENTS OF THE SECOND SESSION

1. The Constitution on the Sacred Liturgy

Our final task is to remark briefly on the accomplishments of this session. As is known, two texts were finally passed after a long series of votes and solemnly promulgated as acts of the Council: the *Constitution on the Sacred Liturgy* and the *Decree on the Media of Social Communications*. The *Constitution on the Sacred Liturgy* provided a legal framework offering basic principles which are being and will be translated into concrete liturgical regulations. This task is being carried out by the post-conciliar liturgical commission, working under the able leadership of Cardinal Lercaro. Regional episcopal conferences also possess a great deal of latitude in applying it in the areas under their jurisdiction. Much has been said elsewhere about the theology, the fundamental practical orientation and the application of this Constitution, so there is no need to speak about it here.

2. The Decree on the Media of Social Communications

As is well known, the *Decree on the Media of Social Communications* did not meet with as much approval as the liturgical Constitution, against which only four fathers voted. In the case of the communications Decree, the final ballot revealed 167 negative votes and 27 abstentions; on a preliminary ballot, 503 fathers had voted no. In view of the total of 1,598 valid votes cast, the two-thirds majority was barely attained. No doubt the text is not what one would expect from a Council. Yet it can hardly be denied that the substance of this text is sound and that its thoughts are open to further development. The significance of a text depends not merely on its wording but equally on

119

Spirit of Vat II

what its interpreters and users make of it. At the very least, and precisely because of its weakness, this Decree provides a continuing challenge. It shows that preparatory studies are needed to enable the Church to speak effectively to the future. This might perhaps provide impetus to work harder in the future on an issue of such importance today.

3. The Approval Formula

The public has given little attention to another important decision taken on the occasion of the final approval of the two texts; this decision may turn out to be very important in future assessments of the value of the Council. This decision lay in the way the pope expressed his approval of the Decrees. This had two parts. The text began: "Paul, bishop, servant of the servants of God, together with the Council fathers for everlasting memory," and ended: "In the name of the holy and undivided Trinity, Father, Son and Holy Spirit. Each and every one of the things set forth in this Decree has won the consent of the fathers of this most sacred Council. We, too, by the apostolic authority conferred on us by Christ, join with the venerable fathers in approving, decreeing and establishing these things in the Holy Spirit, and we direct that what has been

THEOLOGICAL HIGHLIGHTS OF VATICAN II

enacted in synod be published to God's glory. Paul VI, Pope." The significant point is the twice repeated *una cum*—"together with the Council fathers." With this formula Pope Paul brought into being a new type of conciliar law. It precisely expressed the concept of episcopal collegiality which this was to define.

In the late Middle Ages, conciliar decisions were put into effect by popes as papal law. The pope was their legislator and he could modify them as he saw fit. After the conciliarist interlude of the Councils of Constance and Basel, the Council of Florence returned to the earlier pattern. Its Decrees began with the words: "Eugene, bishop, servant of the servants of God, for everlasting memory." The same thing happened at the Fifth Lateran Council and at Vatican Council I. In the latter case, the formula employed read as follows: "Pius, bishop, servant of the servants of God, with the approval of the holy Council, for everlasting memory." In a certain sense the Council of Trent constituted an exception, since the pope was represented there only by his legates. Its Decrees were not confirmed by Pius IV until after the conclusion of the entire Council. For that reason its introductory formula, in which the subject is "The Ecumenical and General Synod of Trent Assembled in the Holy Spirit," does not yet possess full legal force.

In view of this history, it is noteworthy that the formula chosen by Pope Paul superseded one normally in use since the Middle Ages. Paul's formula stressed a new unity between pope and bishops; his formulation was perhaps conceivable only because the conciliar theory was definitely excluded by the definitions of 1870. In consequence it had in 1963 become much easier to freely discuss the truth contained in this theory. In a certain sense, the formula which joins the pope *with* the bishops constituted a synthesis of the early Christian episcopal Council with the medieval papal Council. It also constituted a renewal of the concept of the Church, achieved by returning to early Christian antecedents without abandoning later achievements. Here, too, a positive and affirmative answer was given to the question often raised before 1962 as to whether a genuine Council was still possible after the definition of 1870.

VII

AFTERWORD

Despite so many positive aspects, the second session did not end in the same optimism as the first session had. In marked contrast to the joyful beginning, a sober awareness of the stubborn complexity of

not as joyful & optimistic

human problems increasingly prevailed as the weeks passed. The skepticism of those who feared that in the final analysis all would remain unchanged became more pronounced. More pronounced also was the resistance of those who clung to existing ways and feared change. Thus all of us became aware of the extent to which the Council, which first came to us like an unexpected gift, represented a summons and a challenge to Christianity and especially to Catholics. No Council, however great its impetus, could by itself bring about the renewal of Christianity. It could only furnish an impulse pointing beyond itself to the routine of daily Christian service. The only appropriate conclusion lay in the individual's daily practice of faith, hope and charity.

PART THREE

The Third Session

I

THE FALL OF 1964

A highlight of the Council was reached on September 30 of this year, when the chapter on the collegiality of bishops was passed on the very first ballot by a two-thirds majority—almost against all expectation. Thus one of the Council's first aims—a positive addition to the work of Vatican Council I—was basically fulfilled. Here the Council had passed beyond the stage of tentatively feeling its way and had begun to assume definite form.

When the sessions began, the complaint was frequently heard that the Council suffered from the lack of a concrete mission, that in contrast to previous Councils it had no doctrinal errors to refute or abuses to correct. It was felt that the discussions would cover every conceivable topic and no satisfactory work could be done. Now it was evident how false this widespread earlier impression was, how little the Church really was living in a peaceful state of universal harmony and general well-being, and what tremendous tasks of adjustment confronted it in a time of such rapid ideo-

Council acknowledged that there were problems in the Church

logical change that even the Church could stand fast without the highest degree of intellectual strength and candor. It is perhaps fair to say that the first real task of the Council was to overcome the indolent, euphoric feeling that all was well with the Church, and to bring into the open the problems smoldering within.

In the fall of 1964, then, what concrete problems did the Council face? These problems may be crystallized into the following groups:

Key problems & Q's

1. The problem of divine worship.
2. The problem of centralism in the Church.
3. The problem of relations with non-Catholic Christendom and the ecumenical movement.
4. The problem of new directions in the relations between Church and State, or what might somewhat imprecisely be labeled the end of the Middle Ages, or even the end of the Constantinian era.
5. The problem of faith and science, or, more specifically, the problem of faith and history, which had become a basic problem for faith through the triumph of the method of historical criticism.
6. The problem of the relation of Christianity to the modern ethic of work, to technology, and in general to the new moral problems posed by a technological society.

THEOLOGICAL HIGHLIGHTS OF VATICAN II

1. The Problem of Divine Worship

This may have seemed to the outsider the least important problem. He might have been tempted to see in it a kind of estheticism, a hobby for specialists and historians. But for the Church, divine worship is a matter of life and death. If it is no longer possible to bring the faithful to worship God, and in such a way that they themselves perform this worship, then the Church has failed in its task and can no longer justify its existence. But it was on precisely this point that a profound crisis occurred in the life of the Church. Its roots reach far back. In the late Middle Ages, awareness of the real essence of Christian worship increasingly vanished. Great importance was attached to externals, and these choked out essentials.

The essence of the ancient Christian liturgy in the texts was no longer visible in the overgrowth of pious additions. Luther's protest against the Catholic Church therefore involved a very basic protest against Catholic liturgy, which he denounced as idolatrous. He supplanted it with a simplified devotion concentrated on God's Word. This is not the place to discuss the loss of substance that accompanied this amputation. Without doubt vital members were removed along with diseased ones (as is often frankly stated by Protestant theologians today). But we want to study here the internal Catholic development. The Catholic reaction

129

to Luther's attack took place at Trent. The reaction was on the whole inadequate, even if it did eliminate the worst abuses and make possible a certain measure of rebirth. Trent was content to do two things:

> **(a)** To set forth integral Catholic doctrine, now (at least in regard to the idea of sacrifice) presented in purer form. But Trent did not sufficiently consider the Reformation's genuine problems of conscience, nor did it realize how problematic were the notions of adoration and sacrifice—the two main difficulties of late medieval eucharistic doctrine.
> **(b)** The overgrowth of liturgical non-essentials was cut back and strict measures taken to prevent a recurrence of this.

The main measure was to centralize all liturgical authority in the Sacred Congregation of Rites, the post-concilliar organ for implementation of the liturgical ideas of Trent. This measure, however, proved to be two-edged. New overgrowths were in fact prevented, but the fate of liturgy in the West was now in the hands of a strictly centralized and purely bureaucratic authority. This authority completely lacked historical perspective; it viewed the liturgy solely in terms of ceremonial rubrics, treating it as a kind of problem of proper court etiquette for sacred matters. This resulted in the complete archaizing of the liturgy, which now passed from the stage of living history, became embalmed in the status quo and was ultimately doomed to internal decay. The liturgy had become a rigid, fixed and firmly encrusted system; the more out of touch with genuine piety, the more attention was paid to its prescribed forms. We can see this if we remember that none of the saints of the Catholic Reformation drew their spirituality from the liturgy. Ignatius of Loyola, Theresa of Avila and John of the Cross developed their religious life solely from personal encounter with God and from individual experience of the Church, quite apart from the liturgy and any deep involvement with it.

The baroque era adjusted to this situation by superimposing a kind of para-liturgy on the archaized actual liturgy. Accompanied by the splendor of orchestral performance, the baroque high Mass became a kind of sacred opera in which the chants of the priest functioned as a kind of periodic recitative. The entire performance seemed to aim at a kind of festive lifting of the heart, enhanced by the beauty of a celebration appealing to the eye and ear. On ordinary days, when such display was not possible, the Mass was frequently covered over with devotions more attractive to the popular mentality. Even Leo XIII recommended that the rosary be recited during Mass in the month of October. In practice this meant that while the priest was busy with his archaic liturgy, the people were busy with their devotions to Mary. They were united with the priest only by being in the same church with him and by consigning themselves to the sacred power of the eucharistic sacrifice. Perhaps the clearest example of the coexistence of archaic liturgy and living para-liturgy was the old form of celebration of Holy Saturday. In the morning the liturgical ceremony commemorating the resurrection was celebrated in virtually empty churches. The ceremony had no significance at all for the congregation. In the evening the people had *their* commemoration of the resurrection, with all the splendor of baroque delight in ceremony and display. Between the two ceremonies came a long day of silent remembrance of the stillness of Christ's tomb. Little did it matter that the official liturgy in its ivory tower had begun hours ago to intone the Alleluia.

With the end of the baroque period, the force of the baroque para-liturgy also went into decline, although in some regions it remained very much alive. The endeavors of the Sacred Congregation of Rites to preserve old forms had obviously resulted in the total impoverishment of the liturgy. If the Church's worship was once again to become worship of God in the fullest sense—i.e., for all the faithful—then it had to get away from fixed forms. The wall of Latinity had to be breached if the liturgy were again to function either as proclamation or as invitation

THEOLOGICAL HIGHLIGHTS OF VATICAN II

to prayer. Experiments in "de-Latinization" by smaller groups or through the use of interpreters soon proved insufficient. It was now clear that behind the protective skin of Latin lay hidden something that even the surgery performed at Trent had failed to remove. The simplicity of the liturgy was still overgrown with superfluous accretions of purely historical value. It was now clear, for example, that the selection of biblical texts had frozen at a certain point and hardly met the needs of preaching. The next step was to recognize that the necessary revamping could not take place simply through purely stylistic modifications, but also required a new theology of divine worship. Otherwise the renewal would be no more than superficial. To put it briefly, the task only half finished at Trent had to be tackled afresh and brought to a more dynamic completion.

This also meant that the problems which Luther and the reformers had seen in the liturgy had to be dealt with once again. Not the least of these was their objection to the rigidity and uniformity already evident then in the ceremonies. The point was not, of course, for the Catholic Church to somehow work toward the positions of the Reformation. As we have already said, the amputation performed by the reformers could not supply any model for Catholic liturgical reform.

But the questions the reformers raised could well serve to spur a return to the ancient Christian heritage.

It seemed well worthwhile to honor the positive seriousness of these questions and to see the possibilities they opened up as a help in our own effort for renewal. Both sides have much to learn from one another, and in the work of the liturgical movement this had already in fact happened.

If we view the Council's initiatives for liturgical reform in their historical context, then we may well consider them a basic reversal. The value of the reform will of course substantially depend on the post-conciliar commission of Cardinal Lercaro and what it is able to achieve. The problems and hopes of liturgical reform anticipate some of the crucial problems and hopes of ecclesiastical reform in general. Will it be possible to bring contemporary man into new contact with the Church, and through the Church into new contact with God? Will it be possible to minimize centralism without losing unity? Will it be possible to make divine worship the starting point for a new understanding among Christians? These three questions represent three hopes, all bound up with liturgical reform, and all in line with the basic intentions of the recent Council.

2. The Problem of Centralism

Unlike the problem of liturgy, the problem of papal centralism is readily understandable to everyone. Even the person indifferent to religion sees the papal primacy as an obstacle to the union of Christendom.

The seriousness of the question from the Protestant viewpoint is indicated by the fact that Luther finally characterized the pope as the antichrist. Eastern Christianity, while it does accord the bishop of Rome a primacy of honor, emphatically denies his primacy of jurisdiction. The problem becomes even more complicated in that theological pronouncements are almost always inextricably mixed with ideas and habits of Church policy. Thus it seems almost impossible to make a theological pronouncement which does not have further implications.

The many obscurities of history add to the problem. A few brief recollections will suffice. During the confusing period of migrations of peoples, communications between West and East were to a great degree severed. Rome, which had always ruled as a patriarchate with considerable administrative authority over the regions of the West (even apart from her spiritual significance in the ecclesiastical world), now found herself alone and confronted with the young nations and their newly established Churches. She found herself elevated automatically to a position of almost unlimited central authority. The idea of perpetuating the Roman Empire in a sacral empire tended to further confirm her position and to give it a political character. The opposition that grew up from the late Middle Ages onward was in its turn political. The Councils of Constance and Basel set against the idea of ecclesiastical monarchy the idea of an ecclesiastical parliament, yet still in terms of a centralized Church government. The episcopal movements of modern times, finally, are based on the national idea, which runs counter to the Church's fundamental nature.

In this sense the dogma defined in 1870 represents progress insofar as precisely at the moment the political power of the papacy collapsed, its spiritual essence was reemphasized. At last, after centuries of papal primacy in the political realm, a purely theological concept of the function of the bishop of Rome once more came into focus. Yet the outcome was still dubious in many ways. Theology seemed to lose its freedom in the face of an all too smoothly functioning central teaching office which prejudged every question almost before it had come up for discussion. In its missionary work, the Church had forfeited freedom of action because it was compelled to force all mankind into a Latin framework with which Catholicism seemed to have become identified. Much more could be said about this, not to mention the ecumenical consequences of the definition of 1870.

Vatican Council II tried to move forward in this area by its effort to formulate a genuinely spiritual view of the episcopate as a complement to papal primacy. The Church was no longer seen in terms of political models, but in terms of biblical images. These images became reality at one single point—the point at which the image seemed to acquire its greatest sublimity. This was when the Church was designated as the body of Christ. This was not, as the encyclical of Pius XII (1943) still seemed to see it, simply a clarification of the idea of the Church as an organism. Rather, it views the Church as made up of worshiping congregations. The "body of Christ" is the key phrase, the code name for the content of the Church's liturgical worship, at whose center is the Lord's supper, communion in the body of Christ. Thus the phrase, "body of Christ," epitomizes the idea that the Church exists where divine worship of Christ is celebrated. The fundamental unit of the Church is the congregation worshiping God. This also means that the Church is neither a parliamentary nor monarchical super-State, but rather a fabric of worshiping congregations whose unity consists in the essential unity of divine worship and the faith witnessed to in that worship. In the Council's text, the Church is essentially understood as a fabric of worshiping congregations.

From this viewpoint, too, the ecclesiastical ministries are defined. They thus appear as a plurality of ministries. Ministry in the Church essentially involves presiding over and preaching during the divine liturgy. It therefore involves a ministry of service. It serves as the table of the Lord's supper. A person who presides over a worshiping community is traditionally called a "bishop." Auxiliary functions, such as that of priest (presbyter) and deacon, were later additions. The Church, made up of communities whose function is divine worship, is accordingly built up from a community of bishops, one of whom as successor of Peter is responsible for the unifying function. This is probably the central idea in the Council's doctrine of collegiality. The consequences could therefore briefly be summed up as follows:

> (a) The unifying papal office remains in principle undiminished, although it is seen now more clearly in its proper context. The function of this office is not monarchic rule, but rather coordination of the plurality which belongs to the Church's essence.
> (b) The plurality of the various bishops' Churches belongs essentially to the unity of the one Church. This plurality constitutes the inner structure of the one Church.
> (c) Within the unity of the Church, a relative degree of autonomy belongs to the individ-

ual Churches which normally will consist of a larger group of diocesan Churches. This independence will express itself in liturgical as well as administrative matters.

(d) Thus the first step has been taken to make possible the corporate union of other Churches with the Catholic Church in place of individual conversions. In these corporate unions, the uniting Churches as well as those already united would maintain their identity. They would remain themselves and would be able to contribute their charisms to the Church universal. In other words, the restoration of the plurality of the diocesan Churches within the unity of the one Church makes possible a new ecumenical point of departure.

(e) At the same time a new opportunity is offered for giving ecclesiastical status to Churches separated from Rome.

(f) The scope of freedom within the Church is increasing. Here too, as in the liturgy, the decisive question will be the extent to which the Council's proposals achieve reality in the Church's life. But there is no doubt that the passage of this document by the Council could become a milestone in the history of the Church.

3. The Ecumenical Problem

This problem has essentially been outlined in what was said above. All the work of the Council was in a sense centered on the ecumenical problem. Thus the schema on ecumenism epitomized a leitmotiv of the Council—a new and serious consideration of all problems involving the separated brethren. This involved a readiness to see and admit the mistakes of the past and to make amends for them, and the determination to remove every impediment standing in the way of unity. So much has this concern asserted itself that even conservatives have worked more or less successfully with ecumenical ideas. Sometimes (as in the Council's discussions of Mariology), they completely misunderstood the actual state of affairs. In view of this situation, I want to dispense with further analysis at this point of the text on ecumenism, and instead concentrate on another problem which was one of the focal issues in the ecumenical question—the problem of Mariology.

It was without doubt an explicitly ecumenical decision when the Council decided in the fall of 1964 to incorporate the schema on Mary as a chapter in the schema on the Church. This was motivated not only by the desire to preserve proportion, keeping Mariology a part rather than an independent unit among other independent units. The move also revealed a certain

THEOLOGICAL HIGHLIGHTS OF VATICAN II

theological tendency—to see Mary as a member of the
Church who does not, like Christ, stand before us, but
rather has her place with us and among us before the
Lord, as a representative faithful Christian in the world.

In the text, which replaced an earlier draft, the old
systematic Mariology was to a considerable extent
(though not completely) supplanted by a positive and
scriptural Mariology. Speculation was replaced by
inquiry about the events of salvation history and these
have been interpreted in the light of faith. The idea of
Mary as "co-redemptrix" is gone now, as is the idea of
Mary as "mediatrix of all graces." The text still retains a
vestige of the latter title when it says that the custom
has developed in the Church of addressing Mary as
mediatrix as well as with other titles, but this undoubtedly is very different from saying that she is mediatrix
of all graces.

All this must be kept in mind if we want to assess
correctly the discussion of this topic in the Council on
September 16-18, 1964. It is true that the discussion
here often moved on a very mediocre level and at times
scarcely rose to the level of the average devotional treatise. St. Joseph and the rosary, dedication to Mary and
the devotion to the heart of Mary, the title "Mother of
the Church" and the search for other new titles were
favorite topics of the talks, which did greater credit to
the piety than the theological acumen of the bishops

who delivered them. But we must not forget the fact that voices were heard which for decades we had waited in vain to hear. For example, there was the significant address of Cardinal Léger who attacked the use of Marian superlatives and opposed the title "mediatrix," even in its diluted form. He said that even if the title was not without theological merit, it was nonetheless bound to lead, in daily usage and apart from its Christic context, to misunderstandings. Further, he demanded that the text offer clear safeguards against abuses in Marian piety. Another example is the speech by Cardinal Bea, who likewise argued emphatically against the title of mediatrix, even though he himself had strong associations with Marian devotion. He also called in question the exegesis of a number of hitherto undisputed passages of scripture which had been used uncritically by very highly placed personages in support of Mariology. Above all, there was the important address of Cardinal Alfrink, who exposed the incongruousness of the usual contrast between Marian "maximalists" and "minimalists." He demonstrated the theological defectiveness of these long-undisputed categories. This pointed to the difference between the spheres of devotion and doctrine, which implied a decided criticism of the title "mediatrix."

There should be no misunderstanding. The Council did not aim to slowly but surely dismantle

Marian devotion, and through this to gradually adjust to Protestantism. The aim did however have to take cognizance of the appeal made by separated Christians that the Church move away from a speculative theology that was unmindful of scripture. It had to take a sober and definite stand on the basis of biblical testimony. To see the importance of these proceedings, we must remember how accepted such titles as mediatrix and coredemptrix had already become in theology. Such titles were under the protection of papal teaching, and all contradictory positions were pretty well silenced. The debate, which had been feared by ecumenically minded theologians, can in retrospect be judged a debate which, despite its weaknesses, was salutary and necessary. Only thus could such voices as that of Cardinal Silva Henriquez of Santiago, Chile, be heard—voices which ushered in a new approach to Mariology. This may turn out to be extremely significant. Anyone aware of the prior theological situation, who knows the seriousness of the questions involved, will look back at this sometimes dreary debate, and be grateful.[1]

4. Religious Liberty

The debate on religious liberty will in later years be considered one of the most important events of a

Council already rich enough in important events. To use the catch-phrase once again, there was in St. Peter's the sense that here was the end of the Middle Ages, the end even of the Constantinian age. Few things had hurt the Church so much in the last 150 years as its tenacious clinging to outmoded political-religious positions. The attempt to use the State as a protector of faith from the threat of modern science served more than anything else to undermine the faith and prevent the needed spiritual regeneration. It supported the image of the Church as an enemy of freedom, as a Church which feared science and progress—the products of human intellectual freedom— and thereby became one of the most powerful causes of anticlericalism. We need not add that here too the evil dates far back. The use of the State by the Church for its own purposes, climaxing in the Middle Ages and in absolutist Spain of the early modern era, has since Constantine been one of the most serious liabilities of the Church, and any historically minded person is inescapably aware of this. In its thinking, the Church has stubbornly confused faith in the absolute truth manifest in Christ with insistence on an absolute secular status for the institutional Church. Another characteristic deeply imbedded in the Catholic mentality is the inability to see beyond the Catholic faith, the inability to see the other person's viewpoint; his performance cannot be measured against a standard unfamiliar to him. Yet such habits of thought have characterized Church teaching on the relations of Church and State right up to Vatican Council II.

The Italian and Spanish episcopates, still living under the protection of the State, argued the conservative position. There is no need to deny the sincerity of their concern. They anticipated that the *Declaration on Religious Liberty* would result in a massive sectarian propaganda campaign. The American episcopate, mounting a broad offensive for the first time in the Council, assumed leadership of the opposite side. They were joined by the Anglo-Saxon episcopate, headed by Archbishop Heenan of Westminster, and by the bishops from the mission countries and a part of the South American episcopate. One of the best speeches in the debate was again delivered by Cardinal Silva Henriquez of Chile. France supported this position. It was Archbishop Garonne who frankly broached the issue of the Church's historical guilt and criticized the speeches of the opposition with their constant appeal to previous Church teaching.

We need not oversimplify the difficult problems involved here and picture the conflict in black and white terms. Each side voiced the honest convictions of its conscience. But it was clear that the opponents of the text, who were not opposed to freedom of conscience but to freedom of worship, were fighting for a dying era and that the supporters of the text were really opening up the way to the future. In a critical hour,

Council leadership passed from Europe to the young Churches of America and of the mission countries. It was now as never before unmistakably clear that the Church had become an international Church, drawing on the treasures of all nations and showing the meaning of plurality within the unity of the Church.

This is the place to discuss the development of Council structure. The first session was marked by the complete spiritual leadership of Central Europe, to which the mission countries, the majority of those from South America and a number from North America submitted. These followed an initiative that was new to them. It was one that did not originate with them but that fascinated them and swept them along. Later, however, the balance of leadership shifted noticeably. There was no longer a unilateral predominance of Europe. The other episcopates discovered their independence, so to speak, and carried forward the European initiative in their own way, even though their theologians were mostly European in origin. The two Americas and the mission countries achieved an independent importance and no longer needed European influence to carry forward their demands for renewal of faith in all its aspects.

Finally, we should mention in this connection the *Declaration on the Relationship of the Church to Non-Christian Religions*. Its purpose was not only to clarify

Israel's role in salvation history and the relation between Christian faith and the other religions of the world, but above all to make amends for many centuries of disastrous mistakes in proclaiming the Christian message. It is true that more recent investigation seems to make untenable the idea that the Christian view of the Jews as a deicide people was the actual root and cause of modern anti-Semitism. Nazi anti-Semitism, in any case, attacked Christianity as part of the Near-Eastern and Jewish defilement of the Aryan race. But the guilt of Christians throughout the centuries is nonetheless oppressively heavy. A sweeping purification like that begun by Pope John XXIII still remains as a matter of positive Christian obligation. This, the majority of fathers felt, must not be mitigated merely because bishops living in Arab countries were fearful of disadvantageous political consequences of the Declaration. The Council's norm could not be diplomacy and expediency but only theology and truth.

5. Faith and History

The debate on revelation took up again—this time in a somewhat calmer atmosphere—a problem which in 1962 had set off a most violent controversy: the problem of the historical dimension in theology which underlay the problems of revealed truth, scripture and tradition. This controversy had flared up for the first time about the turn of the century and had led then to the so-called Modernist crisis. The method of historical criticism, which saw the bible in an entirely new light, had won its first victories. The sacred books, believed to be the work of a very few authors to whom God had directly dictated his words, suddenly appeared as a work expressive of an entire human history, which had grown layer by layer throughout millennia, a history deeply interwoven with the religious history of surrounding peoples. By the same token, the deductions of scholastic theology seemed to be doubtful on many points in the light of the bible as seen from the viewpoint of historical criticism.

No less dramatic was the awakening that took place in regard to the idea of tradition. Liturgical forms and customs, dogmatic formulations thought to have arisen with the apostles, now appeared as products of complicated processes of growth within the womb of history. And the very human factors in this growth were becoming increasingly evident. Here arose an enormous danger for the faith. In Protestantism this led to the temporary victory of a liberal theology in which the substance of faith was reduced to a belief in the fatherhood of the Supreme Being and the consequent brotherhood of man. Pius X took drastic measures to suppress similar developments within Catholic theology so as to prevent a similar impoverishing of the substance of faith, but this did not solve the problems.

The schema of 1962 simply reiterated the theology of prohibitions in a very elaborate way. Under different conditions this would have resulted not in the rescue of the faith but in dooming it to sterility, by separating theology once and for all from modern science and confining it in an ivory tower where it would have gradually withered away. Against this attempt the European bishops and theologians rebelled in 1962, for they clearly saw that this kind of defense would suffocate the faith from within by cutting off its air supply—i.e., the possibility of faith's proving itself in terms suited to modern scientific thinking.

The new texts discussed in this session furnished proof that it was possible to present the faith undiminished and yet also to leave open questions which were open scientifically. Even the conservatives had to admit this. They took hardly any serious exception to the new texts. Thus the once dramatic debate now seemed a little wearisome. This should not make us lose sight of the vital breakthrough, however. The possibility of a positive relationship with modern science was demonstrated, despite all opposition, and a broad highway into modern times now began to open up for theology.

6. Faith and the World

Still not yet decided on in the fall of 1964 was the by now almost famous Schema 13, the text on the Church in the modern world.

This was no doubt the most problematical of all the texts, simply because the theological thought needed to achieve a fully satisfactory statement was still lacking. Theology still oscillated between two extremes. There was the enthusiastic affirmation of the world on the one hand, based on the idea of the incarnation (and carried to its most radical point by Teilhard de Chardin), and, on the other hand, a radical theology of the cross, not by any means lightly to be dismissed as Platonistic or even Manichaean. Therefore, expectations were not too high. We will see much more of this later.

There were other problems to which the Council could give no definitive answers. Besides the problem of new directions in Catholic moral teaching, there were also the questions of Christian education (from priestly training to parochial schools) and the reform of canon law (in which mixed marriage reform was not the only issue, although this received most public attention). In such questions, as we will show in detail later on, we have to face up to certain limitations of the Council. Yet it will be to the Council's credit that it faced up to these problems and challenged the future to provide solutions.

One thing was already certain. The Council was fulfilling Pope John XXIII's wish that it make a great leap forward, that it open a window and let some fresh air into the Church. This should not be forgotten, when we review the Council's less dramatic moments.

II

THE COUNCIL AT THE CLOSE OF THE SESSION

We have seen something of the Council situation during the fall of 1964. Further clarification demands a number of observations on the Council situation at this point. In a separate section we shall have to go into the question of the pope and the Council, a question that acquires new importance with the close of the third session. In a certain sense this constituted the most important problem of the third session.

1. Progress of the Council's Work

First of all, the Council's work had moved one step closer to completion. Besides the *Constitution on the Sacred Liturgy*, the *Constitution on the Church* was passed. The *Constitution on Divine Revelation* fortunately survived a series of individual ballots and needed only final passage in the fall of 1965. Of the five Decrees so far definitely projected, in addition to the *Decree on the Media of Social Communications*, both the *Decree on Ecumenism* and the *Decree on Catholic Churches of the Eastern Rite* were passed. The *Decree on the Pastoral Office of Bishops in the Church* had moved to the same point as the *Constitution on Divine Revelation*. It needed only two final general votes for passage. The *Decree on the Apostolate of the Laity*, though badly mauled in debate, was nevertheless generally approved, and after thorough revision was to be put to a series of individual votes.

The texts which were still called proposals met with varying success. Those dealing with religious orders, with the training of priests and with Christian education in general were adopted, though they met with a barrage of proposals for amendment. So these likewise faced only the final balloting. Yet the texts on the priesthood and on the missions were rejected—the latter, as is well known, despite its recommendation by

Pope Paul when he appeared before the general congregation on November 6. Both texts had in the meantime been completely revised and considerably expanded. They were slated for discussion again in the fall of 1965. The draft on marriage, which promised considerable improvement in legislation on mixed marriages and which went far beyond original expectations, was referred to the pope on Cardinal Döpfner's recommendation. For several reasons, this action was welcome at the time.

Though the schema on the Church in the modern world was going through a series of revisions, the debate on this text in the fall of 1964 proved to be a high point in debate up to that time. The frankness, the sober seriousness, the courage and objectivity of the bishops who spoke on such delicate questions as birth control and atomic warfare all had a healthy effect. During this debate there was considerable progress in the discussion of how faith should come to terms with the world, and renewed hope arose that the Catholic religion might be freed from its shell of cold abstraction so that faith could shine forth in all its illuminating power. The two Declarations which had been detached from the text on ecumenism between the second and third sessions met a peculiar kind of fate. Debate had shown that a large majority was in favor of the *Declaration on Religious Liberty*. On the other hand (without a vote it was difficult to determine precisely how large the minority was) the minority was quite vocal. This minority opposition was quite concerned about the Spanish and Italian concordats. These concordats could hardly be considered completely in line with the spirit of this Declaration. Thus the debate turned into a battle over the traditional forms of the relationship between the Church and society. So the text stirred up an excitement which purely spiritual matters rarely arouse, but which becomes unavoidable where concrete existing forms are threatened. Cardinal Bea's secretariat, in its first revision of the text after debate, was understandably anxious to free the discussion as much as possible from emotion, to allay needless fear and to steal the thunder of the opposition by meeting their demands as far as possible. But this well-intentioned appeasement is what proved fatal, for the resultant revision of the text was so complete that it could rightly be said that an entirely new text was under consideration. According to the Council's statutes such a new text would require a new discussion and could by no means be immediately voted on.

This turn of events was in many ways regrettable. It showed the recalcitrance of a theologically untenable position which would only harm the Church. Frankly admitting this—and it must be admitted—we must also add that this text, unhappily rejected, presented its own case very badly. Anyone wholeheartedly in favor of its purpose would scarcely have wanted it passed in the form in which it was resubmitted. This is not merely because of the many compromises which considerably diluted the original statement, but also because of the bad and unhistorical point of departure, based not on the Gospel and what the Church as Church can say with full authority, but on doubtful natural law constructions. Either these really were commensurate with natural law and therefore had no need of further reiteration by the Council, or they did not represent truths arrived at by reason alone and therefore should not be put forward as such. As a matter of fact, the American model came perhaps too clearly through these supposedly timeless natural-law doctrines. Instead of setting up an ideal construct of Church-State cooperation, it seemed better to present the Gospel principle of non-violence with all its consequences, removing the frightful error of St. Thomas who thought it necessary to correct the gospel in suggesting that there is no need to await the day of judgment. Teaching in a closed Christian society, he said that it was praiseworthy and salutary to weed out elements of evil and destroy sinners on our own authority (*S. Th.* 2-2, q. 64, a. 3 c ad 1).

The new discussion of the entire question during the Council's fourth session was therefore to be welcomed. As matters stood at the end of the third session, no Declaration would have been preferable to the inadequate proposed text, for the idea of religious liberty was gathering force. Unless it could be suitably formulated now, there was no hurry. The Council had sufficiently made clear that a Declaration would be possible in the not too distant future. There could no longer be any turning back.

Quite different, and no less unforeseen, was the fate of the Declaration on the Jews. For reasons that were obscure, it had been considerably diluted during the period between sessions. Here too the discussion indicated a clear majority in favor of the original and vigorous theology that had been drawn chiefly from the magnificent chapters 9-11 of the epistle to the Romans. The opposition in this case was quite unmistakably political in character. This once again made the opposition particularly emotional in quality. The obliging attitude shown again by Cardinal Bea's secretariat was of a somewhat different sort than in the question of religious liberty. The Declaration on the Jews was not further diluted, but on the contrary restored in its full force and even somewhat strengthened. However, it was then incorporated into a comprehensive theology of world religions. Dealing with all the large non-Christian religious groupings, it necessarily also took a position on the problem of the ancient People of God. Thus the Declaration on the Jews was turned into the *Declaration on the Relationship of the Church to Non-Christian Religions*. This may not have been the best thing to do. We need only reflect on what St. Paul said of Israel: "They are Israelites, and to them belong the sonship, the glory, the covenant, the giving of the law, the worship and the promises. To them belong the patriarchs, and of their race, according to the flesh, is the Christ...." (Rom. 9, 4f.). These words give the Jews a special place in salvation history and in theology, an image which must not be clouded over. Furthermore, it could be said to be doubtful that the time was ripe for a theology of the religions, despite the urgent need for such a theology.

In any event, it appears that this text profited from all the stir created on November 19 by the rejection of the reworked text on religious liberty. Here too, it could have been asserted with equal validity that a brand new text was under consideration and would have to be discussed anew. As a matter of fact, the new additions were in this case much more far reaching than in the text on religious liberty. Yet there was no such rejection of the text. On the final day of the session, November 20, the necessary individual balloting took place, resulting in definite strong majorities for the various sections of the text. Thus the Declaration seemed assured of passage.

Therefore, the work of the forthcoming final session was clearly outlined. Only four more subjects remained to be discussed: religious liberty, the priesthood, the missions and the Church in the modern world. Ballots of various kinds were also still needed for texts on divine revelation, the office of bishops, the lay apostolate, non-Christian religions, life in religious orders, priestly training and Christian education in general. Consequently there would possibly be more time for discussion in session four, in contrast to 1964. The fourth session would essentially provide for the gathering of the harvest, even though surprises were still possible and two of the four topics still needing extensive debate contained enough fuel to ignite lively controversy.

2. The Pope and the Council

But didn't the Council lose face with the pope's interventions during the final weeks of the session? Didn't even the best texts have a bitter aftertaste due to the impression that in the final analysis the pope could and would do whatever suited him? These were the half-gloating, half-anxious questions heard again and again. To answer them in a way neither cheaply edifying nor grossly oversimplified was certainly no easy thing.

In any case some obvious clarifications could be made. First of all, it could not be forgotten that the pope, as bishop of Rome, was also a Council father and so had at least the same right as any other Council father to help formulate the texts. We know from the ancient Christian Councils of Nicaea, Ephesus and Chalcedon what a decisive role was played by the vote of the bishop of Rome, the bishop of the first Apostolic See. From this viewpoint it was surprising to study the statutes of Vatican Council II and find that, apart from the primacy, the pope's membership in the Council seemed almost forgotten. In any case there were no legal guidelines for ways the pope might bring his opinion into play in the Council. The dangerous disadvantages of this statutory omission were revealed during the week of November 15–21, 1964.

It should also be pointed out that the changes in Council texts originating with the pope (including the shift in emphasis in the collegiality question due to the added importance given the "clarifying prenote") do not basically go beyond the limits of change possible even to a comparatively small group of fathers through their recommendations for amendment. Therefore, caution should be exercised in applying the adjective "docile" to the Council. Such a charge is quite understandable in the heat of the moment, but it does not stand up after a patient and close study of the circumstances. The texts finally passed were in substance the texts the Council had worked out in full freedom, texts which never would have come about without this assembly, and which despite the various dilutions still actually represented the wishes and opinions of this assembly. And the papal modifications were on the whole unquestionably inspired by reasonable motives. All the modifications seemed to follow from the premise that it was the task of the bishop of Rome to reconcile divergent views and to act in this way as an arbiter, seeing to it that peace and harmony reigned in the college of bishops. Even if we doubt whether the measures adopted really serve this aim, this view must be respected as a reasonable application of the idea of papal primacy.

It is certain, however, that no one would want what happened during that week in November, 1964, to ever happen again. For those interventions showed without doubt that the papacy had not yet found a form for the formulation of its position capable, for example, of convincing the Eastern Churches that a union with Rome would not mean subjection to a papal monarchy but rather the restoration of mutual communion with the See of Peter as a See presiding in brotherhood over the many-faceted unity of the Churches of God, knowing no worldly kind of dominion but rather—to use the words of the *Constitution on the Church*—acting as a community in

THEOLOGICAL HIGHLIGHTS OF VATICAN II

the bond of unity, love and peace (n. 22). If those days in November, 1964, brought disillusionment, they showed one thing—namely, that the processes of history take time. The new insights gained in the struggle for genuine episcopal collegiality begin first to gradually take on flesh and blood in the everyday life of the Church; only after this can they develop their full force. In other words, the papal interventions have shown that patience is necessary. Yet they have in no way destroyed the hope without which patience would lose its meaning. The Council, and with it the Church, was on the way. There was no reason for skepticism and resignation. There was every reason for hope, for cheerfulness, for patience. We knew we could go forward without fear, trusting in the Lord who is with his Church always to the end of the world (cf. Mt. 28, 20).

III

ECUMENICAL PROBLEMS INVOLVED IN THE TEACHING ON EPISCOPAL COLLEGIALITY[2]

In its themes the third session was richer and more comprehensive than either of the first two. From among the large number of issues and ideas that seem to invite retrospective consideration, I would like to choose the special problem of episcopal collegiality. Why? I must admit that I have made this choice almost entirely on a quantitative basis. Yet it seems to me that this very quantitative aspect indicates the urgency of the problem. The struggle over the doctrine on collegiality surely occupied more time and attention during the two preceding sessions of the Council than any other issue. No other issue resulted in so much activity both open and covert; nor was any other issue subjected to such a careful and meticulous voting. A few figures will verify this. In the entire schema on the Church, which comprised eight chapters, ten ballots were taken during the first series of votes on chapters 1-2 and chapters 4-8. In contrast, for chapter three alone (the chapter containing the teaching on collegiality) 41 separate votes were taken. The more important sections were voted on sentence by sentence.

However superficial such figures may seem, they nevertheless indicate something of the importance both sides attached to this issue. In view of the heavy emphasis given it by the Council, it seems worthwhile and even necessary, for an evaluation of the Council's trends thus far, to review this doctrine in the light of the guiding principles John XXIII gave the Council at its beginning. These principles the Council had continued to acknowledge as its own. They were the ecumenical principle and the pastoral principle. To put it differently, the question is whether this doctrine of episcopal collegiality has positive ecumenical value and whether it could be called pastoral, that is, promising for the Church's life. Closer investigation will show that both questions are identical in this case. Therefore, we can treat them together as a single question about the ecumenical value of this teaching.

We shall first give a brief sketch of the doctrine on collegiality as set forth in the Council's *Constitution on the Church* (which by now had been passed). This will be done without closer analysis of the pertinent statements which we will simply take as they come to us in a first reading. From these statements a number of ecumenical questions will automatically arise. Also, we shall review those questions which had already been raised on the non-Catholic side. First we shall simply listen to the questions; then we shall go back to the Council texts and try to see what answers it permits us to give.

1. What the Council Text Says about Collegiality

a. *The Text Itself*

The note of collegiality is sounded for the first time in the *Constitution on the Church* when the apostolate of the 12 disciples is described as the foundation and origin of the Church's spiritual ministry. The Council views the basic structure of ecclesiastical office prefigured in the community of the 12, and puts this thought as follows: "The Lord Jesus, after praying to the Father and calling to himself those whom he wanted, appointed 12 who would stay in his company, and whom he would send out to preach the kingdom of God (cf. Mk. 3, 13-19; Mt. 10, 1-42). These apostles (cf. Lk. 6, 13) he established as a kind of college or fixed community, at whose head he placed Peter, whom he chose from among them (cf. Jn. 21, 15-17)" (n. 19). In these few sentences the Council sketched its idea of the biblical basis for office in the Church. It is important to note in this connection that the Council saw the dual character of primatial and collegial office as extending back to the 12 apostles, and beyond that to the will of Jesus Christ himself.

After a few additional sentences further clarifying the basis of the text, there follow a few connecting passages which attempt to demonstrate and explain the continuity of the work of the 12 in the time of the Church, passages which culminate in a sentence which sees that continuity as functioning right up to the present time: "Just as the office that the Lord gave individually to Peter, the first of the apostles, was to be handed on to his successors, so also the apostles' office of ministry in the Church is permanent, and was meant to be exercised without interruption by the sacred order of bishops" (n. 20).

There follows a passage on the sacramentality of episcopal ordination, a topic to which we shall return. After these preliminaries, the actual formulation of the collegiality principle is given. This section of the text (n. 22) was put to a test in a separate vote. It begins with the fundamental assertion: "Just as, by the Lord's will, St. Peter and the other apostles together formed a single apostolic college, so in a similar way the bishop of Rome, as the successor of Peter, and the bishops, as the successors of the apostles, are joined together."

Before the Constitution goes on to draw conclusions from the very carefully considered principle of collegiality, viewing it in terms of its meaning for the leadership of the entire Church, it offers a few historical examples. These of course are not intended as historical "proofs" (which was not the purpose of the Council) but rather to illustrate the meaning of the statement and so offer a kind of interpretation of it. Incidentally, the text underwent considerable expansion at various stages precisely in this respect. In the initial draft simple reference was made to the ancient custom that required the consecration of a bishop always to be performed by three attending bishops. This showed, the previous text said, that it was not merely an individual office that was being conferred in this ordination; rather, the newly ordained bishop was being received for an essentially communal ministry. This reference is still there in the final text but it now only serves to draw attention to the structure of the early Church. The text points out that the early Church lived in the plurality of the various bishops' Churches, which in their mutual communion constituted the one Church.

After this historical reference, to which we shall return, there follows a statement that again leads back to the actual definition of the college. The statement reads: "One is constituted a member of the episcopal body by virtue of sacramental consecration and by hierarchical communion with the head and members of the college." For the time being we will also let this statement stand without further comment and simply go on to the other statements of the text. What follows are the actual and much disputed definitions concerning the function of the college of bishops in the Church—definitions which admittedly do not seem very clear due to the constant tension between full papal power and full collegial power. The text at this point clearly reflects the internal struggle of the Council and the difficulty of arriving at a statement encompassing the whole complexity of history. Whenever one pole is mentioned, this is immediately counteracted by the balancing mention of the other pole. It is impossible to adequately summarize this entire picture within the necessarily brief scope of this report. I shall therefore attempt only to indicate briefly the basic statements in five points.

(1) The college of bishops includes the pope as its head. It cannot therefore be seen as a separate body apart from him, but can be understood only in unity with him. Whenever reference is made to the college, the pope as bishop of Rome is understood as belonging to it and participating in it.

(2) The pope has in the Petrine succession full, supreme and general power over the Church, which he is free to exercise at any time.

(3) The community of bishops is the form in which the apostolic community continues throughout the time of the Church. Therefore, this community of bishops (including the bishop of Rome) also has full and supreme power over the Church, the same power of binding and loosing that the pope has.

(4) In its variety and fullness the college of bishops represents the variety and universality of the People of God. However, inasmuch as it has a common head, it also gives expression to the unity of Christ's flock.

(5) The full power which this college or community of bishops possesses is exercised

in a solemn way in the Council. Therefore, in order to be ecumenical, a Council must be at least "accepted" by the bishop of Rome. Yet the supreme power can also appropriately be exercised by the various bishops scattered throughout the world, in which case the minimum of requisite papal participation is again spoken of as "acceptance."

It seems significant to me that the idea of "acceptance," by its double mention in an important part of the text, is revalidated. In early Church times, "acceptance" was a basic element in the legal life of the Church, and it still is in the Eastern Church. In the early Church (and in the Eastern Church) the usage of the term primarily emphasizes an important element basic to a positive theology of the laity—a theology that does not exhaust itself in fine phrases, but rather assigns the layman an indispensable function in the structure of the Church, in its composition as well as its religious life and its self-realization in the liturgy. According to this viewpoint, a conciliar statement, for example, would acquire its binding force for the entire Church only through the "acceptance" or consent of the entire Church. This "acceptance" was the form under which the faithful participated, very actively, in the development of doctrinal legislation, which was not unilaterally enacted in hierarchical decrees, but rather grew through an intrinsic and mutual interaction between

THEOLOGICAL HIGHLIGHTS OF VATICAN II

the acting function of the bishops and the accepting function of the faithful. There was also an awareness that the liturgical act of the great thanksgiving prayer in the canon of the Mass did not attain its legitimate fulfillment until the attending congregation "accepted" it with its "Amen." Thus the congregation represented most uniquely the function of man in the presence of God's work of salvation—to accept what God had offered. Such acceptance means far more than empty passivity. In the act of open acceptance, human activity reaches its highest power. In losing himself, man finds himself

In our text the idea of acceptance, although used somewhat differently, is still in line with tradition. The text states that although there can be no binding obligation on the entire Church without the pope's participation, yet this indispensable participation may under certain circumstances take place in his simple "acceptance." The history of the early Church again supplies a number of examples of this process. The first Council of Constantinople (381), important for the development of the doctrine on the Trinity, convened without representatives from the Western Churches, yet became a truly universal Council through the "acceptance" of its results by Rome and the West. Such an example may show the scope of the little word "accept." It shows that not all initiative in the Church has to rest with the pope alone, and that the forms under which his primacy functions vary.

These statements represent the nucleus of the doctrine of collegiality; in essence they are reiterated in this section on the infallible teaching office (n. 25). Between these passages, and given far less attention in the discussion, is section 23 which deals with the *mutual* relations of the bishops within the college. In my judgment this text will prove more significant for the ecumenical bearing of the entire issue and the further concrete development of Church life than the much debated statements concerned with the power of the Church as a whole.

b. *The So-Called "Explanatory Note"*

This impression is confirmed by the so-called *Nota praevia explicativa* (prefatory note of explanation). As is well known, this note injected something of bitterness into the closing days of the session, otherwise so full of valiant hopes. A detailed analysis of this very intricate text would take us here too far afield. The end result, which is what we are concerned with, would be the realization it did not create any substantially new situation. Essentially it involved the same dialectic and the same ambiguity about the real powers of the college as the Council itself manifested. Without doubt the scales were here further tipped in favor of papal primacy as opposed to collegiality. But for every statement advanced in one direction the text offers one supporting the other side, and this restores

THEOLOGICAL HIGHLIGHTS OF VATICAN II

the balance, leaving interpretations open in both directions. We can see the text as either "primatialist" or collegial. Thus we can speak of a certain ambivalence in the text of the "explanatory note," reflecting the ambivalent attitude of those who worked on the text and tried to reconcile the conflicting tendencies. The consequent ambiguity is a sign that complete harmony of views was neither achieved nor even possible.

The unsettled situation the Council left behind it was made surprisingly clear in the twilight of the "explanatory note" or "clarifying preamble." On the one hand we find a mentality that looks at the whole spectrum of Christian tradition and the wide scope of possibilities open to the Church. On the other hand there is a mentality which is purely formal in approach and takes the current legal status of the Church as the only standard for its considerations. It therefore regards any change beyond these limits as an extremely dangerous step. The conservatism of this view is based on its aloofness from history and so it basically suffers from a lack of tradition—i.e., of openness to the totality of Christian history. It is important that we see this because it gives us an insight into the inner pattern of the opposing alignments of thought in the Council, often mistakenly described as an opposition between progressives and conservatives. It would be more correct to speak of a contrast between historical thinking and formally juridical thinking. The "progressives" (at least the large majority of them) were in fact concerned precisely with "tradition," with a new awareness of both the breadth and depth of what had been handed down in Christian tradition. This was where they found the norms for renewal which permitted them to be fearless and broad in their outlook. It was an outlook which came from the intrinsic catholicity of the Church.

Let us return to the *Nota praevia*. We noted that its statements created no substantially new situation in regard to the Council text itself. The same holds true for the legal aspects of the note. On the one hand it was set up as the correct guideline for interpretation; on the other hand it was not even incorporated into the Council text itself or voted on by the Council; consequently, it was signed neither by the pope nor by the Council fathers but only by General Secretary Felici. Therefore, it must be said that the bitter taste of this note was not really so much in its content (though that was not too balanced either), but rather in the circumstances under which it appeared.

2. Ecumenical Questions in the Teaching on Collegiality

Here we have already entered the field of ecumenical doubts about the Council's doctrine on collegiality.

These doubts were by no means first raised by the explanatory note, but it certainly brought them right into the open. As a matter of fact these questions had already been raised in the second session and in the interim between the second and third sessions, mainly by Protestant theologians such as Skydsgaard and Maron, as well as by the Orthodox scholar Nissiotis.

The first and fundamental question that had been asked again and again by observers in 1963 ran as follows: As developed by the Council, does the doctrine of collegiality have a solid basis in scripture? Exegetically speaking, can the community of the 12 be rightly termed a "college with Peter as its head"? Or is this not really a later construction, superimposed on the original facts?

Kirsten Skydsgaard, the Council observer from the Lutheran Church of Denmark, expressed this thought in a humorous yet thought-provoking way in a little anecdote. It began with the address of Cardinal Ottaviani on November 8, 1963. In this the cardinal reported that he had asked a famous scriptural exegete just when, if ever, the apostles had actually acted as a college. The exegete replied that he knew of no instance. Skydsgaard then goes on to tell us that he wanted to speak about the matter with a Roman Catholic priest. The priest at first remained silent on the question. They parted, but later on the priest returned with a picture of the crucifixion, on the reverse side of which he had written: "The apostles acted in a collegial way in the Garden of Gethsemane, when they all left our Lord in the lurch." Skydsgaard continued: "We smile, because this was only a story; but suddenly we no longer smile but freeze up. Suddenly all this is very close to us: the denial, the falling away, the cross, but also the resurrection, the gift of grace, the boundless love and power of God. Without this dimension we do not comprehend the mystery of the Church."

The Orthodox theologian Nissiotis was even more articulate in expressing his opposition. Collegiality, he says, "is a very vague expression, with no biblical or historical foundation." Adding a few remarks of a more friendly nature, he comes to his scathing conclusion: "To the Orthodox it is a sign of a dangerous ecclesiological misunderstanding when a Council puts this unscriptural and unhistorical notion of collegiality up for discussion and adopts it."

The second question—no less critical, and discussed chiefly by Gottfried Maron—has to do with the Council's declaration that in the ordination of bishops the "fullness" of the sacrament of priesthood is transmitted. Maron emphatically opposed this Council teaching on the sacramentality of episcopal ordination, referring to Protestant tradition in which he saw a legitimate renewal of the structure of the early Church. He cited St. Jerome as an exponent of this position, although of course Jerome cannot be considered representative in this matter. Maron also referred to the Catholic medieval tradition, the great scholastics, Peter Lombard, Albert the Great, Bonaventure and Thomas Aquinas. Again, a careful reading of these scholastics and a study of their arguments would have indicated not citing them in this connection. (I shall return to this point later.) But the objection remains: Was not the New Testament ministry originally a single ministry? Has not the Church's development of this ministry invested it with an importance hardly justified in view of the evidence from the New Testament and Church tradition, viewed in its totality?

This question finally leads to a third objection, also formulated by Maron, but alluded to by Skydsgaard, Nissiotis and Schlink as well. Does not the doctrine of collegiality signify an intensified clericalization of the Church, a renewal of emphasis on the purely hierarchical element? Will not the barrier between bishop and lay people be raised even higher by the sharper demarcation between bishops and parish priests? This leads back again to the preceding question and shows its concrete significance. For it now seems necessary to delve a little deeper: Is it not the pastors who are the actual successors of the bishops in the early Church, who after all were ministers to their flocks and not remote overlords of entire ecclesiastical regions? Does not the anchoring of the present episcopal structure in the concept of collegiality amount

EPISCOPAL COLLEGIALITY

to a quiet but very serious structural change in the Church as compared with the early Church whose bishops were in a very different situation? Maron in fact maintains this and says: "The Council makes a decided shift in emphasis from the parish and pastorate to a 'Church' in the form of bishops....The result is an ecclesiasticizing and episcopalization of the entire life and worship of the Church, with as yet uncalculated consequences...." In the context of the Council, a peculiar and rather unexpected state of affairs is worth mentioning here. In the debate on collegiality, as far as the doctrine was concerned, a majority of the observers, at least until the beginning of the third session, sided with the curia, although for reasons quite different from those of the curia. This fact leads one to suspect that neither side really fully understood the other. And it shows very clearly that a more intensive dialogue is urgently needed precisely on this central issue if new misunderstanding is not to arise—a misunderstanding that would be especially tragic in view of the good intentions of both sides. Finally, the above described state of affairs also points up the actual weakness of the debate on collegiality. So much energy was focused on the relation of collegiality to the primacy that the intrinsic problems of the collegial principle itself, its complexity, its limits and its historical variability were no longer seen. Every objection was immediately construed as a new assertion of exclusive papal rights and thus any intrinsic meaning the objection

THEOLOGICAL HIGHLIGHTS OF VATICAN II

might have was lost. It is important to see this because an understanding of the prevailing attitudes during the discussion gives a kind of clue to understanding the whole pronouncement and so brings to light its ecumenical meaning.

3. Collegiality as an Ecumenical Task

I shall not attempt to give apologetic answers to the individual questions that have come up, because that would involve very detailed scholarly analysis. It may be more useful and more positive to simply show how the meaning of the doctrine develops from its inner context. Thus the replies to the questions posed will automatically emerge. Of course the weak points too, and what is unanswered in these questions, will also become evident.

a. *The Basis for Collegiality in the Structure of the Early Church*

THE PRINCIPLE OF LOCAL CHURCHES

Viewing the whole complex of thought and ideas underlying the Council's statements, we must first of all admit that this doctrine has its primary and original basis not in an exegesis of the New Testament, but in the rediscovery of the structure of the early Church—

i.e., the still undivided and unseparated Church of the time of the Fathers when the Church was still aware of its direct unity with the apostles. Its structure stood before the Council as a basis for renewal of the structure of the Church in our time. It also influenced the Council's reading of scripture, which it did not interpret in an artificial historical isolation, but "in a forward direction," so to speak, looking to the period of the Church extending from the New Testament to the time of the early Catholic writings. And so, in our attempt to understand the intention of the Council, we must first ask what the structure of the early Church looked like.

Two factors must be considered here. The spiritual ministry which we find still freely developing in the New Testament and not yet fixed, is already apparent at the threshold of the era of the Church Fathers. We see it with Ignatius of Antioch, in the tripartite division of bishop, presbyter or priest, and deacon. The presbyterate and the diaconate were constituted as a college, while the bishop represented the bond of unity in the parish. To understand this correctly, we must not forget that this triple office, with the bishop as its unifying head, reflects the structure of the individual local Churches. This is significant in two respects. First, it makes clear that for the early Christians the first and predominant meaning of the word "Church" was the

THEOLOGICAL HIGHLIGHTS OF VATICAN II

local Church. In other words, the Church was first realized in the individual local Church, which was not merely a separate part of a larger administrative body, but which contained the total reality of the Church within it. The local Churches were not administrative branches of a large organization; they were the living cells, in each of which the *whole* mystery of the *one* body of the Church was present, so that each was simply called *Ecclesia*, Church. I believe that this rediscovery of the local Church is one of the most significant and pertinent statements of the doctrine on collegiality, for it again becomes clear that the *one* Church comprises the plurality of Churches, that unity and multiplicity are not contradictions in the Church.

There is also a second factor to consider. The many local Churches, which taken together are nothing else than the *one* Church of God, are on their part horizontally related. This relationship is expressed in the community between bishop and bishop; that is to say, although the local Church structure is a totality in itself, it is not sufficient unto itself. In its structure as an individual parish it is, so to speak, open-ended. It is complete only when the bishop does not stand alone, but is himself in communion with the other bishops of the other Churches of God.

We see therefore that in one sense the individual Church is a self-contained unity fully embodying the entire essence of the Church of God, but that in another it is open on all sides through the bond of the communion, and that it can maintain its existence as Church only through this openness. The self-containment and integrity of the local Church must therefore not become isolation; rather, it will retain its completeness only in openness, in the unity of communion with the other local Churches.

Applied to our problem this means that while the governance of the local Church is of a monarchical character (although it includes the college of priests and deacons and the cooperation of the entire parish), yet the unity of the entire Church rests on the interrelations among the bishops. This brings us immediately back to our subject. For we are asserting that the office of the bishop in the early Church was related to the community of bishops, and further that the individual bishops could be bishops only in community with the other bishops of the Church of God.

THE PRINCIPLE OF COLLEGIALITY

The word "college," as a designation for this communal character of the episcopal office, dates from the third century. It never was the only word used for the purpose, because the inadequacy of this concept, drawn from Roman law, was recognized, and consequently the term was supplemented by other words such as "order,"

THEOLOGICAL HIGHLIGHTS OF VATICAN II

"body" and "fraternity," all of which more or less refer to the same idea but none of which is really adequate to express it. The Council text in its final form deliberately made use of the various terms. In so using them the Council professed its faith in the internal source of their variety. This variety originally sprang from the awareness that what must be expressed here cannot be defined properly either in terms of Roman law or in terms of contemporary philosophy, because what the Council was confronted with was a new concept that in the final analysis was without any profane parallels. This concept was the communality of the episcopal ministry which had its roots and its essential *locus* in the communality of the Churches comprising the one Church.

NEW TESTAMENT ACTUALITIES

Collegiality thus delimited leads us back to the previous question of how all this relates to the realities of the New Testament. Two points may be inferred from what has been said so far (without claiming to supply the final answer to the whole question). First, I think we must acknowledge that there is an inner correspondence between the unfolding events of the New Testament and the view of the Church as a unity of local Churches mutually joined together through the body and Word of the Lord. We will also find that an interpretation of ecclesiastical office from this viewpoint is in line with the facts of the New Testament. Finally, we must say that the communal character of this office is in fact already outlined in the community of the 12, which was the beginning of the New Testament ministry. To this extent our findings are quite positive. Even though the historical details of the early Church are not traceable to corresponding details in the New Testament, it may nevertheless be stated that early Church structure, which the Council desired to resuscitate with its doctrine of collegiality, was on the whole in keeping with the realities of the New Testament which it carried forward as living tradition.

Once we have conceded this basically positive finding, we cannot deny that there is here a certain abridgement and narrowing. One indication of this may suffice. During the first two centuries of Christian history, Christians of all ranks addressed one another as brother and sister, according to the Word of the Lord: "But you are not to be called rabbi, for you have one teacher, and you are all brethren. And call no man your father on earth, for you have one Father, who is in heaven" (Mt. 23, 8f.). Accordingly, the individual Church communities were called *adelphotes*, "communities of brothers." In the third century this usage underwent considerable change. The first change involved a gradual developing of various "layers" within the Christian fraternity. The ordinary Christian could no longer address the cleric, especially the

THEOLOGICAL HIGHLIGHTS OF VATICAN II

bishop, as "brother," but instead had to address him as "papa." The clergy could address one another as "brother," which meant that this was now a kind of familiar usage reserved for those in higher places. In later centuries, this usage underwent even further changes and involved carefully observed gradations, as is well known.

A second modification even more directly concerns our subject. The word "brother," which has about it that air of simplicity we find in the gospel, was even in its more restricted usage increasingly replaced by the formal title of "colleague," which the bishops now used to address one another. Correspondingly, the concept of brotherhood (fraternity) was replaced by that of collegiality (college). During the fourth and fifth centuries this expression became more and more the customary one for the community of bishops. Other terms coming into use at this time, such as "order" and "body," were also borrowed from legal language and indicated the same development.

In view of these facts, we are tempted to say in regard to the present situation that the collegiality concept is a great gain because the Church assembled in Council rediscovered the basic structure of the undivided early Church. But perhaps there is danger that we will cling to the already somewhat hardened structure of the fourth and fifth centuries instead of following the road to its end and discovering beneath the already completed and juridically fixed "college of bishops" the brotherhood of the whole Church.

Seeing this, we can and must meet the danger that an upgrading of the episcopate may lead to a downgrading of the priesthood and the laity in the Church. This danger can be overcome if the revaluation of bishops is understood at the same time as a revaluation of the Churches of God entrusted to them, represented by them and brought by them into the unity of the whole Church. It is at this point that the idea of collegiality must permit itself to be corrected by the ecumenical idea, or better, to open itself to its full intrinsic potential. The formulations of the Council do not exclude such openness, for their aim was not at all to make bishops into little popes and to increase clericalism. Rather, the Council's goal was to correct the one-sided functions of an overemphasized primacy by a new emphasis on the richness and variety in the Church as represented in the bishops. The Council's statements should be interpreted from this point of view. Its positive ecumenical meaning then will become quite clear of its own accord.

THEOLOGICAL HIGHLIGHTS OF VATICAN II

b. *The Sacramentality of Episcopal Ordination*

Let us move from these considerations to the important problems of the sacramental character of the ordination of bishops. Here too it was not the Council's intention to build up the bishops' self-image or to indulge a fanciful desire to create new dogma. As the text now had established, the Council's statement had no other meaning then to reaffirm the full and independent importance of the ministry of bishops and so to restore the variety and fullness of the Church as against a narrow primatial paternalism. Only in terms of this intention is the real meaning of the Council's statement to be understood. A brief look at the development of the text of the *Constitution on the Church* can make that clear.

Following the initiative of John XXIII, even the draft of the text rejected by the bishops in 1962 attempted to revaluate the office of bishop, and for this purpose submitted two concepts: (1) the sacramentality of the ordination of bishops, and (2) the concept of the college of bishops, which even then was described as the successor of the college of apostles. This second concept was, however, modified at that time by two important qualifications which for all practical purposes obliterated it. These were:

(1) The idea that the college of bishops could exercise its ordinary powers only in an extraordinary manner—namely, in a Council convoked by the pope.

(2) Members of the college of bishops could only be residential bishops. In other words, the requirement for membership was jurisdiction over a particular diocese, conferred by the pope. In the light of this, the college would appear in the long run to be nothing more than an institution of papal privilege, and the great idea of collegiality threatened to evaporate.

In contrast with this obviously inadequate draft of 1962, in which we have both an affirmation of the sacramentality of episcopal ordination as a single isolated thesis, and, on the other hand, the idea of a college of bishops absorbed into the idea of primacy, the present text contains an important passage that combines both ideas and thus invests both with a new significance. This passage also breaches the wall that separated the Middle Ages from the early Church, and hence the Latin West from the Churches of the East. We see the reason why future references to Peter Lombard, Albert, Bonaventure and Thomas Aquinas will no longer be meaningful in this issue.

This passage consists in the inconspicuous little statement that membership in the college of bishops is attained through sacramental ordination and communion with the head and members of the college (n. 22).

THEOLOGICAL HIGHLIGHTS OF VATICAN II

This statement gives episcopal collegiality a double basis but in such a way that these two roots are inseparably connected.

(1) First, a directly sacramental root is established in the very act of a bishop's consecration. For this act concerns not only the individual as an individual, but also his acceptance into a body, his incorporation into a ministry, in which a common bond is essential. In the background appears a renewal of the very idea of sacrament itself. Sacrament is no longer understood as a merely individual gift, but relates to the living unity of Church as organism.

(2) The second root of collegiality is the actual communion with other bishops and the bishop of Rome.

This obviously goes far beyond the thinking of 1962. According to this statement, collegiality is not based on a papally conferred jurisdiction, paralleling the sacrament of ordination as though that sacrament were merely an individual gift; rather, collegiality reaches into the very essence of the sacrament, which as such carries within it an intrinsic correlation to the community of bishops. To render this thought a little more clearly, we may say that two things have been achieved in the new text.

(1) The college of bishops is not merely a creation of the pope, but rather a sacramental actuality—an

autonomous reality stemming from the intrinsic nature of the Church.

(2) The rigid juxtaposition of sacrament and jurisdiction, of consecrating power and power of governance, that had existed since the Middle Ages and was one of the symptoms marking the Western separation of the Churches from the East, has finally been eliminated. A brief historical survey may clarify this.

One of the arguments given in the Middle Ages for keeping these two areas separate was the argument that the eucharist had to do with the *actual* body of the Lord—and that the other sacraments stood in correlation to the eucharist. The power to rule in the Church, however, had to do with the *mystical* body of Christ, and this ruling power was delegated and organized by the pope. Thus the legal sphere became completely independent in the Church alongside the sacramental sphere. There was no mutual interpenetration between the centralism of the law, shaped and administered by the pope, and the pluralism of the administration of the sacraments, dependent on sacramental consecration. Our century's liturgical and theological renewal has removed the basis for this division. We know again today that the sacramental and mystical body of Christ do not exist as parallel separate realities, but have their existence both from and with each other. The eucharist is there to build man up for the body of Christ, and

THEOLOGICAL HIGHLIGHTS OF VATICAN II

conversely the building up of the Church is accomplished through the eucharist. Each of these ministries penetrates the other. Whoever has, as a priest, the privilege of presiding over the eucharist not only transforms the substance of the bread into that of the body of Christ, but is also performing a ministry for the Church of God, which lives from this eucharist. In the eucharistic office, both the sacrament and the "ruling power" interpenetrate one another, and it becomes at once clear how inappropriate the words "rule" and "power" are with regard to the Church. We have no more right to speak of a quasi-profane ruling power, neatly separated from the sacramental ministry, than we have a right to speak of a separation between the mystical and eucharistic body of Christ.

But this means that the pluralism of the sacramental communities and the unity of the Church's ministries safeguarded by the pope likewise interpenetrate one another. It is precisely this that is the actual content of the doctrine on collegiality. Its reference to the sacramental definition of the office of bishop ultimately comes from a sacramentally defined image of the Church. The ministry of the bishop is not an externally assigned "administrative power," but rather arises from the necessary plurality of the eucharistic communities (i.e., of the Churches in the Church) and, as representing these, is itself sacramentally based. The ruling of the Church and its spiritual mystery are inseparable. Only by dealing with this issue in such depth does the text make possible a "decentralization" of the Church that will progress beyond a merely opportunistic organizational change and move into the sphere of genuine spiritual renewal.

c. *Results*

From this we come to a final step which at the same time leads us back to the starting point of our deliberations. The collegiality of the bishops, as a medium for achieving unity and plurality and as an expression for the upbuilding of the one Church of God from the many local Churches, supplies the normal pattern of orderly life in the Church. This collegiality can take many forms. The early Church established the various synods and instituted the patriarchate; today the same reality takes a new form in bishops' conferences. The case where supreme authority must be exercised over the entire Church is rare in the life of the Church. Thus the dispute as to the form the college of bishops could be as an independent form of supreme authority over the entire Church, apart from the primatial form of this power, is really no more than a dispute over a borderline case, and to focus the entire question on this point alone is to involve ourselves in peripheral polemics, losing sight of the real issue. More important is the recognition that a large part of the pope's actual functions originated from the patriarchal position of the bishop of Rome within the Latin region, associated as it was with the primacy. Thus it is really an offshoot of an early Church form of collegial ministry. This insight leads not only to a doctrinal relaxation on the issue, in which obligations of law are by no means always involved, but it also points to the way in which renewal can further progress. The crux of this insight is not the extreme instance of use of supreme authority, which was the concern of the "explanatory note" with its subtle distinctions and of the corresponding sections of the third chapter of the *Constitution on the Church.* Rather, the crux is in the everyday life of the Church, in the normal situation encountered in that life. The real objective will be to learn to treat the normal situations as the proper domain of collegial authority, and not to indulge in hair-splitting subtleties and distinctions in discussion of supreme power.

the spirit of Vatican II?

CONCLUDING REMARKS

A few final words are necessary to sum up the third session of the Council, which has been subjected to so many conflicting judgments.

There is no doubt about it; not everything has been achieved that one might have hoped for. Much remains incomplete and fragmentary, and even what has been achieved, such as the doctrine on collegiality of bishops, is more properly termed a beginning than an end. This task implies many difficulties and also many hazards; it is not a prize to be confidently carried off. We must go even one step further and say that everything a Council decides only can serve as a beginning; its real importance is achieved only in its translation into the realities of every-day Church life. So in any case the question remains as to what degree this translation will succeed. We must realize that any success in this regard may be frustrated not only by the opposition of those who are called, perhaps a little condescendingly, the "conservatives." (Incidentally, their sincerity and the need for their services should not be called in question. I hope it has been evident, at least to some extent, in our discussion that their objections were by no means pointless, but rather in many respects very worthy of consideration.) No, progress may just as easily come to nothing through our own spiritual inadequacies, through our lack of genuine Christian strength. This strength comes from the wellsprings of faith and must be more than an easy acquiescence—a desire to be modern simply because others are.

Perhaps it was salutary that the final days of the third session of the Council brought all these question marks out, and that we have been made aware of the shortcomings of all our endeavors despite any premature triumphalism on our side. On the other hand, a salutary embarrassment (this is what it really was) was certainly not all that was accomplished in two months of common endeavor to discover the proper form of witness to the truth of the Lord in our time.

Anyone who witnessed the three first sessions of the Council and compared them with one another must admit that the episcopate became more open-minded from year to year. From somewhat timid and tentative beginnings, in which a few spokesmen had to carry a whole host of astonished listeners along with them, discussion advanced to the point where in 1964 it became extremely frank and did not evade issues any longer. In the common struggle for truth, statements were boldly made which five years ago would have been virtually unthinkable. Now the entire world episcopate was caught up in a movement, in a unity of purpose that reached from South America to Indonesia and from Europe to Central Africa. This spiritual awakening, which the bishops accomplished in full view of the Church, or, rather, accomplished *as* the Church, was the great and irrevocable event of the Council. It was more important in many respects than the texts it passed, for these texts could only voice a part of the new life that had been awakened in this encounter of the Church with its inner self. Progress may at times have seemed difficult and slow, entangled as it often was in the political devices and disputes, both large and small, which to a considerable degree marked the public image of the Council and often enough its daily routine. But all of this seems trivial and transitory in comparison with the true event—the awakening of the Church. If we keep this in mind we will be full of gratitude for what God has chosen to set in motion through that seemingly so simple old man, good Pope John. Nor will this gratitude diminish when we realize that what has been granted us in this Council involves also a mission and a challenge—one that will require great patience, the patience which comes from faith.

Notes to Part Three

1. It indicates ignorance when sometimes it is alleged that the Council, by adopting the title "mediatrix,"

aggravated the ecumenical situation regarding Mariology. The truth is that the Council reopened to theological discussion the question of Mary's mediating role in grace—which some theological manuals had already declared a doctrine of the Church. The Council also here gave this discussion a new direction.

2 See J. Ratzinger, "The Pastoral Implications of Episcopal Collegiality," in *Concilium*, 1: *The Church and Mankind* (Glen Rock, N.J.: Paulist Press, 1965, pp. 39-67).

PART FOUR

The Fourth Session

I

OPENING OF THE SESSION AND THE NEW SYNOD OF BISHOPS

When on September 14, 1965, the bishops gathered in St. Peter's for the opening of the fourth and last session of the Council, they were in a certain state of concern. They would now have to face the hardest problems, problems which had been postponed for three years— the Declarations on religious liberty and on the relationship of the Church with non-Christian religions, particularly with the Jews. Also on the agenda was the very important draft, ominously titled Schema 13. The first two texts had failed more than once to win final approval, due to powerful forces opposing them. In the meantime it had also become known that the pope himself had strong reservations about these two texts in view of the break with tradition they entailed—and this despite the reassurances of those who defended them. There was no telling how this problem could be satisfactorily resolved. What was most to be feared was that they would be so diluted as to lose all force. Perhaps in that case it would be better to completely drop the texts. Then there was that other problem-child, Schema 13. It had grown to 83 folio pages of Latin text. How could so much material be debated, revised, voted on, revised again, again voted on, finally revised, passed and promulgated, all in a few weeks? This appeared a sheer impossibility, particularly because the text dealt with such difficult problems as marriage and family, war and peace, Church and State: besides, it faced the unfathomable problem of defining the role of Christianity in the contemporary world. Without satisfactory results in these three main problem areas, the last session—and thus the Council as a whole—seemed more or less doomed to be an embarrassing failure, despite all the promise and moments of jubilation.

All the texts had already been discussed. Four of them had been scheduled for further discussion—the texts on religious liberty, the priesthood, the missions and Schema 13. But the remaining work for the plenary meetings seemed rather limited, and the end was in sight. However, for the commissions, work would start all over again, and a great deal had to be done before the final votes could be taken. What were the majority of the bishops, who were not members of any commission, to do in the meantime? Was not the fear justified that the Council would slowly disintegrate, and that many of the bishops urgently needed for final passage would be absent during the voting?

These were some of the concerns that clouded the opening of the fourth session. The mood was in many ways comparable to the uncertainty of the bishops at the opening of the Council in the fall of 1962. As in 1962, so in 1965, the pope's opening address was the first good omen. Encouragingly, the address evoked the wider theological perspective that had been missing in the critical days of 1964. This was very important. Among the noteworthy statements were the following: "Listen! To listen to the mysterious voice of the Comforter will be our first duty in the days that lie ahead." Or again: "In this world the Church is not an end but a means. It serves all mankind." And, above all, there was Pope Paul's view of the Council as committed to the law of love. When a historian would in the future ask what the Catholic Church did in this age, the answer, the pope said, would have to be, "It loved." From the final address of December 7, we can perhaps infer that it was this thought that made it possible for the pope to approve texts he had at first viewed with doctrinal reservations. In that final address he again reviewed the objections which not only conservatives but also some of the observers had meanwhile raised against the Council's "modernism." Pope Paul found the answer in the formula that "the religion of this Council was primarily the religion of love." This, said the pope, was also the answer to the objection that the Council had defected from the gospel. "The Lord said, 'By this shall all men know that you are my disciples, that you love one another'" (John 13, 35). The primacy of love overcomes doctrinal doubts. It justifies the Council. Let us add now a word from the pope's speech on September 14, which also shows with how little illusion the pope understood love: "The art of loving is often converted into the art of suffering. Should the Church abandon its duty to love because it has become too dangerous or too difficult?"

But more important to the fathers than this basic tone of the pope's address, which once again affirmed the spirit of the Council, was the new reality which this speech created: the long-awaited synod of bishops, whose eventual establishment some had already begun to doubt, was now officially constituted. The following day, the general secretary read the pope's *motu proprio*, giving legal form to this new organ of service in the Church, thus making tangible reality what had for so long been mere wish and hope. The news was not greeted with the enthusiasm which could perhaps have been anticipated. The bishops had become too disillusioned for this by the time of the fourth year of the Council. But it was enough to revive an almost lost opti-

THEOLOGICAL HIGHLIGHTS OF VATICAN II

mism and to recreate the spiritual climate which had carried the Council forward during the years of its work. This climate was more than ever needed during this period of final effort. Against the constitution of the synod, published on September 15, it had been argued that it nowhere mentioned the idea of collegiality, as the majority of bishops had hoped it would. This new body is, in the words of the *motu proprio*, "directly and immediately subordinated to the authority of the bishop of Rome," who, moreover, is the only one who has the right "to convoke the synod, whenever it appears to him opportune, and also to appoint the place of its deliberations." It was said that this showed a profound difference between the synod, as conceived by the Council, and its papal realization. A collegial organ had been turned into an instrument of the primate to use as he wished. Undeniably there are differences. The Council's *Decree on the Pastoral Office of Bishops in the Church* developed the idea of the synod of bishops—to use the now official title—as essentially coming "from below," from the concept of episcopal office and from the bishops' responsibility for the whole Church in virtue of their office. But the papal *motu proprio* sees the synod as coming "from above," from the papacy, which now needs more than ever to be linked with the bishops. However, this difference is only relative, and it logically follows from the different points of departure of the two documents. The

Council's Decree on bishops was worked out by bishops commissioned by the assembled bishops of the Council. Thus it moves from the viewpoint of the bishops, and it moves toward the center—the common service of the universal Church. The papal text, conversely, begins from the primacy and moves toward the bishops. The fact will be more important than the theoretical structure. If the synod, kept by its direct subordination to the pope from subordination to the curia, can succeed in going beyond routine concerns of daily administration to make the living voice of the universal Church heard and make its effect felt at the center of the Church, then its basis will make little difference. Whether it makes its first appearance under the aegis of collegiality or as an aid to the primatial office will be of very little importance. The primatial office will in any case take on a new aspect, if the pope's brother-bishops are included in his own ministry. Thus, even if anonymously, collegiality will become part of the picture of the primacy.

We may think it unfortunate that the pope retains the exclusive right to convoke the synod. We are reminded here of the corresponding formula of the so-called "explanatory note," added in 1964 to the third chapter of the text on the Church.[1] But we must not overlook two surprisingly positive aspects of the structure of the new synod. (1) Most of its members are elected by the bishops, not appointed by the pope. That is, they are chosen in a collegial, not a primatial fashion. This expresses the idea of collegiality. (2) The name itself, "episcopal synod," gives a special weight to the synod. The term "bishops' council" would have no theological character, and the whole body would have seemed an ad hoc institution without any spiritual significance. The term "synod" reflects the structure of the early Church, which did not yet know the later isolation of the monarchial episcopate. Rather, it sees the bishop as connected with his priests on the one hand and fellow bishops on the other, joined together in regularly held synods. In fourth-century Byzantium, this model was the basis for patriarchal synods, which resulted in the institution of standing synods. This meant that the patriarch did not govern his region in a monarchic but in a synodal way. He governed in community with a group of bishops, all of whom together formed, so to speak, a kind of permanent small council. Thus, on the patriarchal level, the monarchic principle was integrated with the collegial. The term "synod" thus anchors the new body of bishops in these ancient traditions. Therefore, it cannot be considered the mere product of contemporary utilitarian ideas. Rather, it has been elevated to express an element of the Church's constitution which must always be present in this or that form to supplement and correct the monarchic idea.

The establishment of the synod of bishops at the beginning of the final session was also an answer to the question which became increasingly urgent as the Council went on: What would happen after the Council? Would the case be dismissed, and would we return to our everyday routine as if nothing had happened? Or would ways be found to make the Council's influence felt in all areas of the Church—"in head and members," as the late Middle Ages expressed it? If we may say that the synod is a permanent Council in miniature—its composition as well as its name justifies this—then its institution under these circumstances guarantees that the Council will continue after its official end; it will from now on be part of the everyday life of the Church. It will be no mere transitory episode, but will be able to mature what was sown in the often stormy days of the sessions.

II

THE FIRST TOPIC OF DEBATE: RELIGIOUS LIBERTY

The Council began by discussing for the third time the draft on religious liberty. No really new statements could be expected in view of the prolonged previous struggle. There still were those who wanted the whole question discussed solely on the level of abstract truth and error. They could rightly insist that error does not have the same right as truth. Yet the counterargument still stood. This was not a problem about truth or error but about the coexistence of people in whom truth and error are often intermixed. People certainly cannot live together if they assert what they think is truth by means other than those consistent with truth. Another area of conflict remained. Religious liberty was still seen as irresponsibility toward truth. This of course was objectionable. Against this it had to be repeatedly reiterated that religious liberty implies no diminution of the sacred responsibility of conscience and of the human mind toward truth. Nor did liberty diminish the seriousness of God's call, contained in his saving revelation, or make God's demands on men optional. Rather, the problem was to clarify the way in which God's call comes to man—as an appeal to his free choice, which alone can respond to God's call in love, saying "Yes, I do." The third objection to the text drove even deeper. This objection had only crystallized during the second discussion of the text. Even the supporters of the text now felt its urgency. Was the text not based too exclusively on a concept of natural law which lacked sufficient scriptural foundation? The allegation was that the scriptures said nothing of the subject, and that it therefore had to be treated entirely on the basis of tradition. It was easy to refute this by pointing to the fact that the whole New Testament was written under the sign of the cross, not the sign of worldly power. The New Testament testifies to God's weakness in that he chose to approach man not with legions of angels but solely with the gospel of his Word and the testimony of a love ready to die. Then, too, Jesus' whole life was a struggle to communicate true understanding of his messianic mission, as against official Jewish misunderstanding. The story of the temptation as related by Matthew (4, 1-11) and Luke (4, 1-13; cf. also Mk. 1, 12ff.) exemplifies this struggle and exposes the later Jewish political interpretation of the Old Testament and its messianic hope as a diabolical temptation. To this Jesus opposes his new spiritual understanding of the hope of Israel.

The temptation narratives represent the struggle over the correct understanding of the Old Testament which was the central issue of Jesus' dispute with the official Israel of his time. The idea of a messianic king of this world is unmasked as the offer of the prince of this world, demanding the adoration of his power. The shadow of this temptation emerges again in the narrative of the multiplication of loaves in the desert; here the same scene is reenacted (cf. esp. Jn. 6, 15) and Jesus' reiterated refusal, with the cross already looming in the background. From this point on in all the evangelists the fatal end of Jesus' struggle appears increasingly inescapable (Mk. 8, 27-30; Jn. 6, 60). There could be no more devastating condemnation of the attempt to use external force to assert the gospel than appears in the "Get behind me, Satan" of these texts (Mt. 4, 10; cf. Mk. 8, 33, addressed to Peter!). Who would not be reminded here of the terrible accusation of Dostoievski in his "Grand Inquisitor," set against the background of the temptation story? No matter how unjust or unfair its perspective, it raises a question of grave seriousness.

Here, however, we have considered only the negative aspect of religious liberty—the non-violent character of the Gospel. The schema positively proclaims freedom of worship and of belief, not only for individuals but also for religious communities within the framework of public good order. This is in line with the social character of human nature, and thus in line with all truly human religion. All this can be inferred from scripture, yet it really goes beyond the biblical horizon. Here a Latin American bishop, Muñoz Vega, offered an idea worth further consideration. The freedom Christian faith claims for its missions presupposes freedom of religious testimony in general. A faith which demands, on the basis of its claim to universality, universal freedom to preach its message to all nations in the midst of their traditional religions, must also affirm freedom of belief as a basic religious form. Otherwise it would contradict itself. Thus the idea of mission provides the intrinsic basis for the idea of religious liberty, and this liberty is visibly and intrinsically involved in what is most fundamental in the revealed Christian message. It is therefore all the more scandalous that so much prodding from the de-Christianized world was needed to make the Church realize and recall what belongs to its own nature.

All this reflection went on with great earnestness during the third discussion of the draft on religious liberty, from September 15 to 21. Although very little that was new came to light, there were nonetheless some great moments. One outstanding example of this was the speech of Cardinal Beran. He had suffered for years in prison for his faith, but was now able to participate in the Council. He was a free man again, although an exile from his country. Beran arose and gave his unconditional support to the text on religious liberty, pointing to the history of his country where violent suppression of the Hussite movement had inflicted wounds on the Catholic faith that still have not been healed. Force used to promote faith injures nothing so much in the long run as this faith itself. This was the impressive lesson taught by Beran's speech. It could be documented from examples other than that of Czechoslovakia. Another climax came when Cardinal Urbani of Venice endorsed the text on behalf of a group of Italian bishops, thus breaking down the hitherto united front of the Italian episcopate. Thus the three-year struggle gradually neared its end. It was a struggle that needed time to develop the idea at issue; the third round of debates was really necessary for its final clarification.

Thus the text was almost unanimously approved in the last voting of December 7, 1965. There were only 70 negative votes and 8 abstentions. Nor can anyone say that the text lost any of its force in comparison to previous versions. It did accent three things more strongly than previous drafts: (1) the unchanging claim of the Catholic Church to be the only true religion; (2) the uncompromising character of truth; religious liberty is a matter of social and political coexistence, which does not affect man's relation to truth but only affects truth's historical concretization. Freedom is a vulnerable thing, which can easily destroy itself if used without restriction. Freedom itself demands that the freedom of the individual be protected against the abuse of freedom in its many forms. Such a requirement, however, can lead in turn to the disregard of freedom. There are no sure norms or standards here. The text sought to formulate the limits of the idea of public good order, and to define them in such ways that any restriction on freedom is distinctly seen as a means to protect freedom. (3) Most controversial was the third newly emphasized aspect. The text attempts to emphasize continuity in the statements of the official

THE FIRST TOPIC OF DEBATE: RELIGIOUS LIBERTY

Church on this issue. It also says that it "leaves intact the traditional Catholic doctrine on the moral duty of men and communities toward the true religion and the only Church of Christ" (n. 1). The term "duty" here has doubtful application to communities in their relation to the Church. Later on in the Declaration, the text itself corrects and modifies these earlier statements, offering something new, something that is quite different from what is found, for example, in the statements of Pius XI and Pius XII. It would have been better to omit these compromising formulas or to reformulate them in line with the later text. Thus the introduction changes nothing in the text's content; therefore, we need not regard it as anything more than a minor flaw.

III

THE STRUGGLE OVER SCHEMA 13

1. History of the Text

The main achievement of the final session was the debate on Schema 13, which was passed on December

7 as the *Pastoral Constitution on the Church in the Modern World*. The longest of the Council's documents, it also was one of its most important results. Therefore, it requires some detailed analysis.

The history of the text begins in late fall, 1962. In a way typical of classical Roman scholasticism, the preparatory commissions had suggested a kind of codification of all present theological thinking on the issue. They wanted clear and cautious formulations. But caught in the web of system, ideas lost in force and vitality as they gained inner perfection and clarity. The prepared text did definitely broach topical contemporary questions. One of the texts treated Christian ethics in general; another dealt with marriage and the family. But their solutions were too pat to be convincing. They were marked by an assurance which had no basis in revelation, and by an authoritarian decisiveness which is simply no longer suited to the complexity of reality. They were put in categories that came more from classical antiquity than from Christianity. Marriage was discussed in terms of the basic category of "end"; its morality was deduced abstractly from the concept of nature. Here social utility was viewed as overriding the reality of the human person. The whole emphasis was on asserting and reiterating the rights of the Church. The Church's ministerial function was virtually forgotten.

It will be recalled that the first of these texts—the draft on divine revelation—led to a general vote of no confidence. This in effect repudiated the kind of theology that characterized all these draft texts. The rejection of the proposed draft as inadequate also implied a demand for a fresh start. The reversal had profound and exciting implications. What was at stake was not this or that theory, this or that special scholarly question, but the form in which the Word of God was to be presented and spiritually interpreted. Here the preparatory effort was unsatisfactory, and the Council rejected the extant texts. But the question at this point was: What now? This is when the fathers got the idea of preparing a single comprehensive new document which would treat all the topical questions involved in the Christian relationship to the world. This schema on the Church in the contemporary world would take positions on such questions as marriage and the family, war and peace, and so on. Cardinal Suenens, Cardinal Montini concurring, drafted a new overall program for the Council. This saw the Council's work as concentrating on the subject of the Church. The first objective was to deal with the Church's intramural problems; the second phase of work would deal with the Church's relation to the world outside.[2]

The program was easier to draft than to implement. Not until late 1964 did the Church and world text begin to take shape. Its chief architect was the German moral theologian, the Redemptorist Bernhard Häring. A draft mainly written by him was submitted for Council discussion in the fall of 1964. The draft's basic idea was a result of the events which had shaped it. It said that authoritarian *fiat* had to be replaced by dialogue, insistence on rights by an awareness of the Church's duty to serve. Instead of social utility, personal values needed emphasis; instead of the familiar theological notion of abstract nature, there had to be a revaluation of the concrete realities of man and his history. From these leading ideas, three chapters on general Christian anthropology were worked out, as well as a fourth chapter which dealt with concrete problems—marriage and family, war and peace, social questions, the relation of the Christian to culture and modern technological civilization.

The first basic difficulty of the text was that it was really a two-part text—the schema proper and the so-called addenda. These treated the issues of the schema again, sometimes more precisely. This fact alone made another complete revision necessary, in which the two parts would be integrated. Other defects were that many of the statements were rather vague, and that two lines of thought ran confusedly counter to one another. The text on the one hand was intended to be biblically rather than scholastically and philosophically oriented.

215

On the other hand, the text was intended to come sympathetically to terms with the contemporary situation and modern thinking. The result was that the text wound up neither biblically precise nor really in line with modern thought. The debate on this draft had yielded only a general approval of the direction and the aim of the effort. Yet the fathers also ordered a thoroughgoing revision of the text.

In January, 1965, a group met again in Ariccia, near Rome, to commence work on this. In the meantime, the press secretary of the French bishops' conference, Abbé Hauptmann, had drafted a new text which prevailed over another draft of Polish origin. The French text was certainly more fluent in language than the Polish draft, but its theological precision left much to be desired. The Germans, who had brought no draft of their own, had to content themselves with criticizing here and there and suggesting amendments. The basic text remained as was. In the following months, the text went its way through the various phases of commission work, and by the end of the summer it was ready for distribution to the fathers.

2. The Schema of the Fall of 1965

The schema began with an analysis of the contemporary historical situation. Then it went on to

THEOLOGICAL HIGHLIGHTS OF VATICAN II

develop (in its first part) fundamentals of Christian anthropology. Here too were treated the problems of atheism and of the meaning for man of technology and history, the problem of Christian hope as compared to secular hope in our time, and finally the position of the Church in the contemporary world. The second part, which leaned more on Häring's draft, was again devoted to specific problems. It treated extensively the meaning of science and its autonomy, political life, international community, aid to underdeveloped countries and related questions. The text as a whole ran, as noted above, to 83 Latin folio pages. Obviously a document of this size could not have been worked out with the needed precision; it was too large for any real discussion.

When, in the fall of 1965, the first private soundings were followed by debate, it became clear that the old conflict of "integrists" and progressives promised to break down. No longer was there the old majority and the old minority; new lines had formed to face new tasks and new problems. True, the integrists had meantime formed a solid organization—the so-called *Coetus Internationalis Patrum* (International Alliance of Fathers), whose main supporters were Bishops Sigaud of Brazil, Carli of Italy, and Lefebvre, General of the Order of the Holy Spirit. This organization saw the Council speeches of Cardinals Ruffini, Siri, Santos and Browne as a model for their work at the fourth session. They were remarkably active. On a number of issues, especially the texts on religious liberty and the relationship with non-Christian religions, the *Coetus* acted as a tight bloc of about 200 fathers. But on Schema 13 it could no more take a uniform stand than could the progressive group—where a certain conflict between German and French theology began to be visible. Naturally there were men of variant or even conflicting views on both sides.

a. *Structural Problems in the Text*

The first textual problem lay of course in its language. The text, translated from French into Latin, had been thought out in French and so was hardly intelligible in Latin. The limits of Latin became evident when facts and circumstances, alien to the world in which Latin developed, had to be expressed. The Latin world, with which the Latin language will be forever associated, is not exactly the world of today. The historical barriers of language could not be surmounted without contortions.

More serious were the problems of content. There still remained the conflict which had marked Häring's schema—the dichotomy, we might say, between biblicism and modernity. Both tendencies had been able to join forces in opposition to a systematic and one-sided neo-scholastism, for the texts originally prepared under scholastic auspices had neither been biblical nor in harmony with modern thinking.

Those who favored a modern viewpoint should easily have seen that openness to the radical humanity and earthiness of biblical thought and speech naturally led to an openness to authentic human realism and thus automatically to modern thinking, speaking and questioning. Those who favored the biblical viewpoint should in turn have seen that the modern breakup of the scholastic system led naturally to an openness to the primitive source of theological thinking—the bible, which is so human precisely because it is so permeated by the divine.

Therefore, no one will deny that there is good reason today for an alliance between biblical and contemporary thinking. But at the Council it became equally evident that these two tendencies do not simply coincide and that their harmony cannot be taken for granted. The biblical world has a historical reality we cannot adopt as our own without its inner transformation. Nor can our world be seen in terms of its biblical foundations without a profound analysis of its hidden inner powers and their origin. The chief concern of the text was to speak to contemporary man; thus it had tried to express fundamental theological ideas in a modern way, and in doing so got even further away from scriptural language than did its scholastic predecessors. Biblical citations were little more than ornamental. This not only made the text difficult from an ecumenical point of view, but also made it questionable for modern man. What interest could an outsider find in a theological statement which had largely divorced itself from its own origins? A pastoral question must be added: What hope could possibly be placed in a reform which sought to satisfy everyone?

It should be clear by now that the dichotomy between biblical and modern theology has a direct bearing on the problem of theological language. The French theologians who had drafted the schema defended their idea as follows: We want to speak to contemporary man. Therefore, we cannot begin immediately with ultimate theological considerations. We have to begin instead with what is understandable and accessible to all, what we have in common, and move step by step from there. We must not serve up too much scholarly jargon; we must leave the shelter of our theological ghetto and expose ourselves directly to reality. We must not keep hiding from harsh practicalities behind the fixed walls of our special studies.

Certainly this is basically sound. It is one of the main responsibilities of contemporary theology to step out from behind the protective walls of specialized jargon and to face directly the challenge presented by living man. But the way this was worked out in the proposed text was something else again. The text set out reasonably and politely, as though eager not to frighten anyone away prematurely with unexpected theological ghosts. Yet at the end it had to embarrassedly admit that there were other things that had to be mentioned. Besides the very plausible idea of man as a being called to subdue the world and free to decide his own fate, there is also the christological idea that man is saved by Christ alone.

So what the method involved, after all, was that only some of the statements were dejargonized—those statements, that is, which Christian theology makes in common with humanism in general. But the characteristic and proper message of the Church, its statements about Christ and his work, were definitely left in the icebox of frozen and fixed terminology. The contrast made the properly Christian message seem just that much more unintelligible and obsolete. The question is now inescapable: Just what does redemption mean? What meaning does all this theology have for man, since man can be adequately described without it? One easily got the impression that the authors themselves saw the christological and centrally Christian statements as only acceptable on faith, that they considered this world of faith a kind of second world alongside the first and immediate world of ordinary daily life, and that they felt that people should not be prematurely and unnecessarily bothered with the second world. But looking at the text objectively, it was necessary to say: Either faith in Christ really concerns the center of human existence, either faith is something definitely realistic that goes down into the far reaches of the human heart so that the person who accepts faith can only here begin to describe man realistically, or else the world of faith is a world separate from the ordinary world of experience. But how then could faith make its claim on the center of man's existence? Doesn't this really reduce faith to an ideology for those who need such a refuge apart from reality? If theology is really going to move out from behind the walls of specialized science, it must be courageous enough to do this wholeheartedly. It must not in the name of caution leave its finest values hidden there. The debate on this text taught us that lesson.

Apart from the conflict between the biblical and the modern view, between theology as a science and a religious proclamation that would directly reach contemporary man, there was another problem which was no less relevant to the contact between faith and the world of today. This could be called the dilemma between the two claims of faith and of freedom in dialogue. The schema, in opting for dialogue, had assumed a way of speaking in which faith seemed to be a kind of

THEOLOGICAL HIGHLIGHTS OF VATICAN II

recondite philosophy. It seemed to deal with things we really knew very little about but wanted to know more about—things we perhaps should know something about because they involve our destiny. But faith is essentially certainty; it gives men firm ground to stand on, while knowledge offers no more than probability. This approach was of course well-intentioned; the idea was not to disturb the dialogue. Here faith was seen as a conversational search into obscure matters. But the conversant, the partner in the dialogue, really knows that the man of faith does not actually think matters are as obscure as all that. The man of faith could not really think so if he really believed. This apparent search and inquiry would seem deceitful to the conversant if he recalled that doubt is not the object but the opposite of faith. Here it was astonishing to see the text sometimes becoming imperative and demanding about secular matters, even where there was no need for this. What was also discomfiting was the rather dubious use made of the term "People of God"—as if the People of God looked with pity and compassion on other people's problems and was not itself made up of frail, human beings, as though the People of God were one socio-logical group among others, looking for contact with the other groups. Here the claims of faith were scaled so large as to be profoundly distorted.

We can grant that it was very difficult to compose an adequate text on this because there was no experience and no model on the doctrinal level for a Christian dialogue with the world beyond the realm of faith. There had been from the beginning only two kinds of doctrinal pronouncements—the creed of obligation and the anathema of negation. Both kinds of pronouncement made sense only within the realm of faith; they were based on faith's claim to authority. Since the beginning of the modern era there had been increasingly smaller circles of people ready to bow to the authority of the teaching Church. There resulted an increasing need to develop a form of expression which might be valid beyond the narrow circles of believers. But this form had been developed in strict analogy with the intra-Church pronouncements. Pronouncements directed to the world typically employed language of authoritative ordinance. The only difference was that the new statements presented themselves as interpretations of natural law. They thus claimed to be valid for all men. Yet very little consideration was given to the fact that acceptance of a natural law interpretation from the Church implied a recognition of its authority. Thus acceptance required commitment and obedience to the Church which only faith can attain. The more authoritative the pronouncements sounded, the less they were really likely to reach listeners outside the Church.

224

No doubt it was to the Council's credit that it was aware of this problem and that it looked for a new non-authoritative form of pronouncement. But another distinction should have been made between pronouncement and dialogue. The first would have been to replace authoritative imperatives with the proclamation of the Gospel—thus opening up the faith to the non-believer and abdicating all claim to authority other than the intrinsic authority of God's truth, manifesting itself to the hearer of the message. This attempt would have necessarily involved translation—meaning an effort to make the message intelligible to the listener on his terms. Here the problem of dialogue would have reemerged—a dialogue which, without denying the claim of the gospel message, would yet be cognizant of the intelligibility of the message and its limitations. Preachers of the gospel themselves often enough do not see distinctly that their understandings of the world and of faith have become so inseparably intermingled that they do not distinguish the two. It is an open question whether the final text really succeeded in finding an adequate form for addressing the world. But the effort alone must be rated an important accomplishment and a step in the right direction. Moving away from a posture of authoritative imperatives, the Church has returned to a mis-

sionary posture, relying much more on the unpreten-
tiousness of simple language.

b. *Faith in the Technological World?*

The basic division on this schema concerned a
problem so far only touched upon. This was the problem
of the basic relationship of the Christian and the Church
to the technological world. From the thinking of Teilhard
de Chardin, a position seems to be developing today
which seeks to solve the problem by identifying to a high
degree Christian hope with modern confidence in
progress. Seeing the progressive process of hominization
as a process of christification, seeing the cosmic Christ as
the point Omega toward which the entire evolution
moves, this view identifies the end of technological
development with the completion of christogenesis.
Here technological utopia and Christian hope in the
kingdom of God merge into one. The pursuit of a tech-
nologically improved world appears as a directly
Christian activity—as preparation for the kingdom of
God itself. Here the reconciliation of Christianity with
modernity seems to be complete. The schema of course
had avoided such an oversimplified interpretation,
which, though it does not do justice to Teilhard's own
thought, does remain operative as a Teilhardian tendency. As far as the Council's schema is concerned, there

remained, despite all disavowals, an almost naive progressivist optimism which seemed unaware of the ambivalence of all external human progress. It was certainly very positive in that it drew back from the posture of medieval suspicion of technological civilization. In this it made a move of decisive historical importance which had not been retracted. But we must also recognize that suspicion is not completely allayed until we have freely and without illusion examined the negative and retrogressive aspect of progress and have honestly measured the distance between technological and human progress. But the crucial question goes even deeper. It could be put this way, for example: What is the relationship between technological progress and Christian hope? The solution presented by crude Teilhardianism is, as noted above, the identification of both. The weakness of the schema, to speak bluntly, was that it did not sufficiently dissociate itself from this view. No doubt technology offers men in many respects something like a redemption. Many things man looks for from faith he now looks for from technology—the conquest of sickness, hunger, cold, heat, poverty, age and even death. And this is a hope not only for the individual himself but for all humanity. Technology offers a hope splendid enough to attract a person to put his whole life at its service. So we are forced to ask what Christian hope means in comparison to this. As we saw above, Teilhardianism, using a cosmic christology, has interpreted technological progress as, for all practical purposes, christological progress, thus calling the Christian into the whole-hearted service of technological progress. But even in its modified form, as found in Schema 13, it was obvious what a horrible perversion of Christianity this represents. Thus, for example, statements about Christian expectation of the world to come were here and there mixed up with technological hopes. Most important, the schema as a whole tended, in its definition of the relationship between the Christian and the technological world, to see the real meaning of the christological in the sacred aura it confers upon technological achievement, rather than developing the christological on the very different plane of the passion of human life and human love.

Perhaps one specific term can help make more clear what is meant here. The schema speaks of the victories of mankind, and means by this the phases of technological progress. The scriptures also know the language of victory, but what they mean is the victory of faith, of love, which the Song of Solomon describes as stronger than death. The New Testament responds to this by revealing the figure of Christ in whom love proves stronger than death—in his willingness to face death by execution on the cross. The New Testament presents the cross as the great victory of Jesus Christ, through which one man really vanquished the world so as to become Lord of the entire world (Phil. 2, 4-11). Thus Christianity cannot mean a sacral transfiguration of the technological. Rather, it reveals a realm which the technological cannot redeem. It remains true in the end that the world is not redeemed by machinery but by love. The connection between the Christian and technology does not come through sacralization of technology but only through the idea of love seen without illusions. Technological service becomes Christian when it is motivated by a service which seeks to humanize men—that is, when it serves love. Then and only then does technological progress serve Christianity and only then is it really progress. The Christian message cannot have as its purpose the glorification of the technological. The technological needs no such glorification. Yet the Christian message should establish critical norms by which to judge the technological.

c. *Question and Answer in Schema 13*

So far we have indicated something of the backdrop against which the discussion of Schema 13 moved. A number of very complex specific problems were also discussed—marriage and the family, Church and culture, the Church and social problems, war and peace, and the development of the community of nations. The reason we have discussed these problem areas in principle is because the same questions remained questions even after the text was passed. The Council could not possibly have intended to clear away at one fell swoop all that was involved in the relation between faith and contemporary human existence. What was important in the Council's discussion of Schema 13 was rather that it recognized these problems and moved toward solving them. We must go on from there.

Almost more important than the solutions offered by the text is the attitude behind the text, which discovered here a new way of speaking. The Council had the courage to produce a public document that did not claim to be inclusive but rather sought to begin a task that would continue. In this basic attitude, the Council, after its difficulties in the beginning and despite many unsatisfactory statements, again found its unity. The great majority of bishops were jointly able to affirm this point of view, and they carried the Council with them, so that in the end resistance came only from that comparatively small group which generally felt the spirit of the Council to be an abandonment of Christian tradition and thus dangerously mistaken.

3. On the Final Text of the Constitution

Even though we must still discuss the *Pastoral Constitution on the Church in the Modern World* in terms of its problems and its openness, yet it would be wrong to stress this aspect alone. Despite its preliminary character, the document offers comprehensive orientations which must be briefly considered in a concluding survey. Since the document was increased to 85 pages of Latin text (two pages were added), it would be beyond the scope of this study to give anything more than a sketchy presentation. We will therefore confine ourselves to a consideration of three examples of the methods and procedures of the Constitution in order to give some idea of the character of the resultant work in its attempt to deal with the problems and questions of contemporary man.

a. *The Christian and the Technological World*

The first example will continue with the basic question examined above, i.e., the relationship of the Christian to the technological world, treated in the third chapter of the first part ("Man's Activity throughout the World"). The text begins by formulating the problem (n. 33). It points to the new historical situation in which a variety of human cultures are being superseded by a common technological civilization, leading to an increasing unification of mankind. Characteristic of this situation is the fact that technological application of scientific insights has given man an entirely new kind of power over the world. This in turn implies a new orientation toward human existence, based on the opportunity to make things functional in the service of man. But this alters the basic relation of man to reality. He now views reality essentially from the functional point of view. He no longer approaches the world from the viewpoint of contemplation and wonder, but as one who measures, weighs and acts. Thus religious mystery largely vanishes from things because this mystery cannot be methodologically examined. The attitude of the expectant suppliant gives way to an attitude of conscious responsibility for man's own destiny. Faced by this situation, the Council does not bemoan and deplore it; rather, it begins by delimiting its own sphere of competency. The text says that faith offers men directive guidance about their origin and destiny (n. 33). But this does not mean that the Church has ready answers for all specific questions. Rather the Church links its own search—a search in faith—with the search of mankind for solutions to these specific problems. The text then goes on to affirm that the new attitude is basically legitimate. There was an insertion in the following section of the text (n. 34) to the effect that an attitude which candidly considers things as things corresponds more closely to the concept of creation and is welcome as a repudiation of a magical view. Latin American bishops, involved in a struggle against magical distortions of Christian faith, had asked for this insertion. They recognized their best ally in the sober scientific view which divests things of magical glamor. The objectivity of science is much more in line with the idea of creation than a false divinization of the world which science and faith equally reject. In the final text this insertion was eliminated, but the meaning is retained in a reference to the idea of creation. The scientific view of the world, which presupposes both the world's non-divinity and its logical and comprehensible structure, is profoundly in accord with the view of the world as created (and thus non-divine): the world as produced by the Logos, God's Spirit-filled Word. Thus, like the Logos, the world is rationally and spiritually structured. One might even say that only such a basic attitude makes natural science possible in its full scope. In this context, a statement begins to make sense which would otherwise sound like cheap apologetics: "This makes it clear that the Christian message does not draw people away from the building up of the world or move men to neglect the welfare of their fellowmen; rather, it moves them more strongly to dedication to the task" (n. 34).

In a subsequent passage this idea is developed into an explicit doctrine on the autonomy of the secular. In individual chapters of the second part this idea is taken up again and applies to the realms of science and political life.[3] The text does not refrain from pointing to the Church's past misunderstanding of these fundamentals, and in a footnote it refers to the case of Galileo (note 7). The results can be summarized in the maxim that Christian action is action in line with the nature of things, without a wrong immediate regulation by the Church which would contradict the innate integrity of things and which would obscure the difference between the Church and the kingdom of God. The Church is temporal and limited in its competence in secular matters. Of course these positive statements do not stand alone, and they must not stand alone, because the technological world, as we remarked earlier, also has its problems and dubious aspects. To decipher the physical structure of things is not the same thing as to decode the meaning of existence itself. Rather, it introduces us to the enigmatic character of existence in its full mystery and thus shows us the riddle of our own existence. Why discuss all this? Because from such problems as these the properly Christian sphere comes into view—not in competition with technology but concerned with the basic human questions which the technological world gives a new place to without being able to eliminate them. What is authentically Christian reality first comes through in a text-sentence based on a quotation from Gabriel Marcel: "Man is more important in what he is than what he has" (n. 35). "To be" and "to have" appear as two distinct categories of human existence. But "being" is the authentic area of human decision-making which remains unchanged through all vicissitudes of "having." Against the background of such permanence the ambivalence of such progress looms large. Progress makes increasingly possible both human self-destruction and genuine humanization. There is about progress, then, an eerily two-faced quality. Technology does not decide whether progress works to salvation or destruction; this decision comes from some other source (n. 37). Thus a perspective opens up which looks toward the only redemptive force—the saving power of love. Love finds its guarantee ultimately only in him who is essentially love: he who not only *has* love but *is* love.

b. *Teaching on Marriage and the Family*

A second example of the approach of the final text is the discussion of marriage and the family (nn. 47-52). It is, of course, quite impossible to present all details of the Council's statement on this complex subject. We will merely try to indicate some of the newer developments that this document contains.

To understand the type of moral theology that has been dominant in Catholic teaching hitherto, we must consider the circumstances from which it developed. The New Testament does not contain a fully elaborated moral teaching, but only a number of concrete imperatives plus an overall reorientation showing the antithesis between law and grace. As far as specific moral statements are concerned, the New Testament remains sketchy. Moreover, the law-grace dichotomy, far from providing a point of departure or an elaborate ethical system, really shows the limitations of any moral theology. This is probably the reason why early Christianity, in working out its concrete moral norms, largely resorted to contemporary models of ethical thought for guidance. It leaned chiefly on the Stoic ethic. The recourse to classical antiquity, and especially to Stoic philosophy, resulted in the emergence of two chief principles in Christian teaching on marriage.

(1) There developed a view of marriage which was essentially "generative" in outlook—generative in the double sense that marriage was entirely subordinated to the *genus humanum*, the human race as such, and was thus subordinated to human procreation in the social sense. From this viewpoint, procreation pertains to man as a being of his particular kind, and as such has nothing to do with any individual or personal consideration. This generative approach largely rele-

THEOLOGICAL HIGHLIGHTS OF VATICAN II

gates marriage to the biological level, seeing it chiefly as a means to the end of procreation. Thus the concept of the end supplies the basic norm for judging marital ethics. Thus a terminology which sees procreation of offspring as the primary end of marriage has until now characterized the classical positions of Catholic moral theology and canon law.

(2) The basic approach of Stoic ethics, despite all its sublimity, can be termed naturalistic because the Stoics saw in nature the directive activity of the Logos; the natural order revealed an all-pervasive divine meaning. Accordingly, the Stoics considered the over-riding moral norm to be nature; a thing was right if it was "according to nature" (*kata physin*).

The moral teaching of the Church largely follows Stoicism in this, so that we may say that both the pro-creative function of marriage and the habit of judging "in accordance with nature" constituted the dual dowry bestowed by the world of antiquity on Christian marital morality. Up to the present these principles have determined the categories of Catholic moral theology.

With this as a background, we can begin to see the great significance of the fact that the *Pastoral Constitution on the Church in the Modern World* eliminated both these categories. Neither the concept of the "prime end of procreation" nor the concept of marital behavior "according to nature" has any place in the

Constitution. This elimination of ancient categories was the result of struggle and effort and clearly marked a radical turn toward new modes of moral teaching, and a turning away from forms that have up to now characterized moral theological tradition. The procreative view is here supplanted by a personalistic view, which of course must not overlook the essentially social meaning of marriage if it is not to become one-sided in the other direction.[4] Even more important is the fact that a moral teaching whose norms came "from below" (from a concept of nature that was not all that unequivocal) was now supplanted by a teaching whose norms came "from above," from a spiritual view of marriage and family. And so, the text points to conscience, to the Word of God, to the Church interpreting the Word of God, as proper guides for morality in marriage.

We may, of course, ask whether the change was no more than a verbal change. Would the recourse to the Church's authority not have the practical effect of leaving everything as it was, despite all the new verbiage? Though this objection is not entirely unjustified since it points to the text's avoidance of the concrete problem of birth control, yet it does not do justice to the text as a whole. There is a decided difference between a total moral statement based on the concept of the race and the propagation of the race and on the concept of "accordance with nature," and a view which focuses on individual conscience, on the Word of God and on responsibility toward children, toward the husband or wife and toward the community of mankind. The context within which conscience operates, the entire atmosphere in which all decision and moral commitment is made, differs radically in these two cases. It is simply not the same, whether a person asks himself if his actions are "in accord with nature" or whether he must ask whether his actions are responsible actions in view of other persons with whom he is related in the marriage community, and whether his actions are responsible in view of the Word of the personal God who has indicated the fundamental pattern of conjugal love by comparing it with love for the Church as exemplified in Christ (Eph. 5, 25-33).

c. *Teaching on War and Peace*

A third example here is the much debated question of the Church's position on modern war (nn. 79-82). As before, we cannot try to cover in complete detail all the statements of the text. We shall only try to clarify the text's structure and to indicate what is actually new and forward looking. Catholic moral theology, beginning with Augustine, and again relying on classical philosophical ideas, sought to submit war to moral norms by developing the doctrine of the just war. But the classical norms for a just war had become thoroughly doubtful in the entirely different situation of modern war with all its horrors. Yet it would be no less perilous and oversimplified were we to condemn all the political leaders and the citizens who agree with them, who still conscientiously see defense of ultimate values as a moral necessity. As a result, a profound dilemma faces the Christian people—a moral problem which distinctly underlines the basic dilemma which the doctrine of the "just war" did not eliminate but at most covered over. In view of the real nature of war and the forces that war unleashes, we must say that any war must be condemned in that, properly speaking, any war is so terrible a thing that it is difficult to see it as at all connected with justice. Yet at the same time the alternative—i.e., complete defenselessness—is also unrealistic. This would no less give rein to universal injustice. The problem comes into sharper focus if seen in the context of atomic weapons. These questions are as a result of recent discussion still fresh in everyone's memory.

In this situation the Council did not deem itself authorized to issue unequivocal and final directives on the application of modern armaments, although with Pius XII it branded as criminal a use of modern weapons to indiscriminately destroy entire cities or

THEOLOGICAL HIGHLIGHTS OF VATICAN II

regions.[5] Rather, the Council moved away from the static definitions of the "just war" theology which presumes to determine once and for all what is and is not morally right. Though such a definition would have the advantage of being concrete in its prohibitions, it would, on the other hand, label as just the merely licit a very dubious procedure. In view of the new situation, the Council moved away from the static morality of the just war toward a dynamic morality of emergency. It recognized the intricacies of the present situation, in which what ought to be is often impossible. Here the alternative, "all or nothing at all," for all its seeming rectitude, turns out to be ultimately destructive of all moral effort. Therefore, the attempt must be made to approach as closely as possible what is morally desirable. Thus we can at least assert moral demands, even though we cannot achieve our ultimate moral objectives. This kind of procedure is wholly in harmony with the pedagogical approach of God as revealed in the scriptures. We recall that Jesus, in explaining the marriage legislation of the Old Testament to the disciples, pointed out that Moses permitted divorce, although it was in conflict with the original order of things, "on account of the hardness of your hearts" (Mt. 19, 8). Such obduracy which makes confessions necessary to get man going on the road toward meeting his moral obligations is not limited to the Old Testament. The degree to which the problem is still with us is especially clear in the problem of war and peace.

It is within this context that the statement is made that the aim must be total peace, a peace which converts swords into plowshares, and in which all war is banned (n. 78). But we have not as yet progressed so far that this can be achieved. Our moral aim, then, must be to do everything we can to make this possible. We must respect international law, further treaties aiming to humanize warfare, denounce recourse to arms wherever possible, respect conscientious objectors (providing a substitute service, if possible) and work for disarmament and for the establishment of an international authority. We must draw the line against the unequivocally criminal, and we must appeal to political leaders to realize the immense responsibilities involved in the possession of modern weapons. In this difficult problem, the text appeals to the conscience and responsibility of the experts and those entrusted with national responsibility. There is no appeal to abstract norms (n. 80).

We may think this result rather meager. But the situation is, after all, full of ambiguities, deficiencies and impossibilities. I feel that, despite its vagueness, the text is good in that it attempts to do the possible. Thus it actually achieves more than would be achieved by a demand for the impossible. Again, as with the question of marriage and the family, I see progress in the structure of the text. It does not presume to set timeless norms for questions so complex in their technological, political and historical ramifications. Rather, it stirs up a feeling of inadequacy about the merely licit. It sees the "licit" as no more than a very temporary concession in a history that finds man still in progress and still very far from doing what he ought to do, very far from doing what is genuinely right.

If we meditate on the Council's statement, we become immediately aware how suited it really is to lead us from what seems to be an almost secular consideration into the very heart of Christianity. The whole of human action is shown to be abysmally deficient when we begin to confess that our moral attitude in this matter, and actually in all other matters as well, is far from what it should be. We recognize that the small righteousness we manage to build up in ourselves is nothing but an emergency morality in the midst of our radical unrighteousness. We are directly and forcefully reminded of St. Paul when we find ourselves forced from behind our shell of protective speculation, forced to admit that our righteousness is nothing but a temporary expedient in the midst of unrighteousness. We find ourselves crying for mercy to him who makes just the unjust. The sincerity of the man who acknowledges reality with no excuses is itself a hidden appeal to the mercy of the mystery which has appeared to the faithful in Jesus Christ. The foremost intention of the Council was to reveal this need for Christ in the depth of the human heart so as to make man able to hear Christ's call. The Council has attempted to put the ministry of faith at the service of mankind in a new way in this historic hour. It has tried to serve God in serving men, to serve God who in himself chose to become a man.

IV

THE COUNCIL'S TWO FINAL DISCUSSIONS

1. The Basic Problem of the Schema on the Missions

The discussion on Schema 13 lasted until October 8. But on October 7, debate on the new text on the Church's missionary activity began. We will not attempt here to present the details of this rather sizable text which, unlike the preceding year's draft, was given a friendly reception. Its six extensive chapters tried to supply a new theological foundation for the idea of the Church's missions and to redefine the role of the missions. We may here briefly indicate the background of the problem. The crucial issue, which gravely affected the whole context of the question, especially for the missionary bishops, was the crisis in which the very idea of missions found itself. The cause of this crisis lay in profound changes in modern thinking about the necessity of missions. The motive which had driven missionaries in the past to bring other people to Christ had increasingly lost its urgency. What drove the great missionaries at the beginning of the modern era to go out into the world, and what filled them with holy unrest, was the conviction that salvation is in Christ alone. The untold millions of people who suddenly emerged from unknown worlds beyond the horizon would thus be hopelessly doomed to eternal ruin without the message of the Gospel. Therefore, the sacred obligation of the faithful to preach the Gospel everywhere seemed the most compelling responsibility of brotherly love, since love not only concerned particular earthly needs, but the destiny of all men. What was involved was either eternal salvation or eternal damnation.

Meantime, in recent generations, the idea had more and more come to prevail that God can save and wants to save all men even though outside the Church, although ultimately not without the Church. This idea was hitherto only applied by way of concession and exception. Moreover, in recent times a more optimistic interpretation of the meaning of the world religions has been propounded. Here, again, closer reflection will once more demonstrate that not all the ideas characteristic of modern theology are derived from scripture. This idea is, if anything, alien to the biblical-thought world or even antipathetic to its spirit. The prevailing optimism, which understands the world religions as in some way salvific agencies, is simply irreconcilable with the biblical assessment of these religions.[6] It is remarkable how sharply the Council now reacted to these modern views. During the debate on the parallel passages on the text on the Church, it had seemed more amenable.

In any event there are very serious problems here. For example, there is the question whether missionary activity should not await a more appropriate time. Might not an attempt to "Christianize" at the wrong time destroy customs and traditions which might better be left to develop to the point where they could be supplanted by something higher, rather than be suddenly undercut by a preaching of the Gospel at the wrong place and the wrong time? Such a preaching would destroy rather than build. Beyond this inner missionary crisis is an external one. It has become clear that the implantation of Christianity in Asia has so far failed. Conversion to Christianity has so far, for all practical purposes, meant conversion to Europeanism. Thus it has been limited to marginal areas of the Asiatic mind. A Christian faith which wants to be and really should be the universal religion of mankind has been unable to genuinely move beyond an Occidental culture. To this hour there has arisen no really indigenous Asiatic Christianity reflecting a genuine grasp of the spirit and culture of the Orient.

Here is where the missionary crisis becomes most urgent. A most remarkable feature of our era of history is the fact that another European world religion has succeeded very well in taking root throughout the world. The Marxist idea has conquered the world. It has done this by ignoring all the theories of adaption and cultural implantation and adjustment which have been so much a part of missionary theology. It has been carried forward on the compelling dynamism of its new promise. In a time which sees the growing unification of mankind, religious divisions are an anachronism. Quite apart from the theological question of the eternal salvation of the individual, the inner dynamism of history and human existence requires as a foundation of missionary activity an awareness that the destiny and salvation of men is a destiny and salvation within history. If it is a fact that human history moves relentlessly toward unification of mankind, then this unification must not be a mere economic unification through technological achievement. It must become a unification in view of human values, a unification of the spirit and of what is highest in the human spirit, its relationship to God. A unification which is not a unification in spirit would lead mankind to ultimate self-destruction through a conflict between external cooperation and inner antagonism. In evaluating the need for the spiritual dimension of the historical process, the atheistic sector, which calls itself materialistic, thinks on a much higher level than some Christians do. If such insights, which see Christianity not within a narrowly individual perspective but rather on the level of historical interaction among men—if these insights are pursued to their logical conclusion, then we might be astonished to see how necessary missions are even today for the salvation of mankind.

This one small hint may suffice to indicate what great problems are involved here, problems which concern not only the theologian.

2. The Schema on the Priestly Ministry and Life

The question of how the Church views the priestly ministry may not seem particularly important to the non-theologian. But when we reflect that in actual historical reality the fate of the Christian religion depends on how well simple priests in their parishes perform, either opening the faith to people or cutting them off from it, then the importance of the question becomes obvious. The text submitted to the Council met with much criticism. Many details of it had not been worked out with adequate care, and here and there it was rather naively conceived. Yet I think that the basic conception represents a fundamental advance, especially from the ecumenical point of view.

Luther's protest against the Catholic notion of priesthood was really based on the fact that in the Catholic view the priesthood was almost exclusively a sacrificial priesthood. In fact, even in patristic theology and especially in medieval theology, the old association between *sacerdos* and *sacrificium*, between priest and sacrifice, had been emphasized again in contradiction to the view of the New Testament. The medieval view saw the priesthood fundamentally as an office charged with conciliating an offended God. The incontestable weakness of this position was that in its effort to find universal concepts, it gave insufficient attention to the special historical character of the New Testament priesthood. It went too far in conforming Christian priesthood to the general idea of priesthood as found in the history of religions. It is true that the idea of reconciliation was raised to a new level. In pagan religions, the idea of reconciliation can go to the point where the priest pacifies the divinity so that there is nothing to fear from the divinity's power. Thus the non-priest was only indirectly concerned with the gods. Though the Christian idea of sacrifice excluded such notions, the one-sided point of departure remained as a very dubious heritage.

Luther's rejection of the medieval interpretation of the priesthood is associated with his critical attitude of all the Church's ministries. Yet it is this misunderstanding of priesthood, and the continuing influence of the misunderstanding, that makes it so extremely difficult for the Catholic Church to find a suitable formula for the place of the layman in the Church. This also affects the total picture of religious living within the Church.

The schema on priestly life and ministry has now eliminated the one-sided emphasis on the idea of priesthood as sacrifice. It moved instead from the idea of the People of God meeting together, so that priesthood is seen fundamentally as service to faith. The text says: "It is the first duty of the priest to proclaim the Gospel of God to all" (n. 4). This comprehensive, fundamental and uniquely Christian perspective results in a correct view of the fundamental act of Christian worship—the eucharistic act, which is basically different in its whole structure from pagan worship and sacrifice. "The eucharistic action is the very heartbeat of the congregation of the faithful over which the priest presides" (n. 5). This means that the eucharist is not simply a self-centered act of consecration and sacrifice performed by the priest, as though it were irrelevant whether lay people participated in it or not. The special commission of the priest in the eucharistic celebration is instead described in the text, in line with the New Testament and the oldest traditions of the Church, in the term "presiding over." In other words, it is the priest's task to serve as a *pater familias*, a father of the family, and to say grace over the Lord's supper on behalf of God's own household. He also proclaims with thanks the death and resurrection of the Lord, and in this glorifies God. He makes present what once took place through the preaching of the Word here and now. He makes Christ's sacrifice present by virtue of the authority conferred upon him sacramentally. Thus the preaching of the Gospel, the sacrifice, the consecrating of the offering, the gathering of the congregation, the glorification of God and the sharing at the table of the Lord in the eucharist are seamlessly interwoven. Here is true religious service and worship, going beyond antecedents from other historical religions. To clearly see all this we must add another dimension. If worship, the preaching of the Gospel, the offering of sacrifice and the gathering of the congregation all merge with one another, and if this interaction determines the scope of the priestly ministry, then there

251

can no longer be any separation between worship and life. So true is this that St. Paul used specifically liturgical terms to describe the ministry of Christian life and suffering. Even in the one passage where he describes his own work as priestly action, he specifies this kind of service: "To be a minister of Christ Jesus...in the priestly service of the Gospel of God, so that the offering of the Gentiles may be acceptable, sanctified by the Holy Spirit" (Rom. 15, 16). The Council's Decree explicitly refers to this text and thus again places the idea of priesthood and worship within its larger overall biblical perspective (n. 2). If the perspective of this text is correctly interpreted and applied during post-conciliar work, then it will have far-reaching consequences for both the ecumenical dialogue and the further growth of Catholic self-awareness.

The public at large, of course, gave hardly any attention to these thoughts. There was much public concern with the fact that the pope forbade debate on priestly celibacy, ordering instead that only written opinions, directed to himself, would be acceptable. This ordinance was occasioned by the proposal of a group of South American bishops to apply to the priesthood the decision of the previous year permitting married deacons. They felt that where deacons did not meet the needs of the Church, married men should be ordained priests. In retrospect we must concede that the climate of sensationalism that surrounded the Council, as well as the resultant restiveness among the faithful, would not have provided the proper atmosphere for a calm discussion of so difficult a problem. In view of the shortage of priests in many areas, the Church cannot avoid reviewing this question quietly. Evading it is impossible in view of the responsibility to preach the Gospel within the context of our times.

V
THE LAST PHASE OF THE COUNCIL

On October 16, 1965, the period of continuous discussion in St. Peter's ended. The plenary congregations recessed for eight days. They convened again during October 25-27 in order to deal with a few more items of unfinished business and also to hear the views of a pastor on the schema on priests. This terminated the period of debate. In three public sessions the harvest of the Council was reaped. On October 28, the *Decree on the Pastoral Office of Bishops in the Church*, the *Decree on the Renewal of Religious Life*, the *Decree on Priestly Training* (an excellent text, by the way), the *Decree on Christian Education* (unfortunately, a rather weak document), and, surprisingly early, the *Declaration on the Relation of the Church to Non-Christian Religions* were all passed. The fact that this latter text (which was an expansion of the originally so-called schema on the Jews) was able to pass with 2,221 affirmative votes against 88 negative votes and 2 abstentions was, in view of all the opposition, an important event. True, the final text appears in some respects somewhat weakened. The great basic statements, however, remained unchanged. And compared to everything that previously existed in regard to the relation between the Church and Israel, it really was a new page in the book of Catholic-Jewish relations.

The next public session, held on November 18, was notable for the fact that, among those who concelebrated the Mass together with Pope Paul, there were such men as Henri de Lubac (who had suffered so much in connection with repressive measures against the so-called new theology) and John Courtney Murray (the chief architect of the schema on religious liberty). In this way the liberty text was given, so to speak, advance public confirmation. That day produced the *Decree on the Apostolate of the Laity* which attempted to formulate a new view of the layman in the Church, and the *Constitution on Divine Revelation*. It was an earlier text on revelation which was the occasion for the first struggle in the Council for the revision of doctrinal viewpoints in 1962. The revelation problem had followed the Council through all four years of its work. Up to the last minute the discussion on this text had been persistently dramatic. The pope himself acted on October 19 in proposing three changes in the draft. During the discussion of these changes, it became evident, by the way, that the collaboration of the pope in work on the development of the text—a collaboration which had caused such surprise in the fall of 1964—had gradually become a method of collegial cooperation between pope and bishops. The pope's suggestions were in this case, as well as in others, submitted to the commissions for final voting and were openly discussed and in some ways profoundly changed. The pope's intervention, which was initially criticized (and properly so, because he had initially acted without much circumspection), involved his taking part in the intrinsic formation of the texts as well as in the confirmation of them. But, as it developed, this intervention had a rather mellowing effect on the papal image. The whole affair had seemed to open up a new style of cooperation between pope and bishops—a style reflected, by the way, in the Council's confirmatory formula. Thus the term collegiality can have a very concrete application in the actual relationship between pope and bishops.

Between the two public sessions, and also after them right up to the end of the Council, the commissions worked at high speed to complete the final text in time for the final series of ballots. Between vacations and voting days, plenary sessions were fitted in during which the reports of the commissions and the reading of the final versions of the text were heard. There was one more dramatic moment when (November 9-11) the comments of the bishops' conferences on an extra-conciliar draft on the simplified granting of indulgences were read. There was no trace of the spirit of the Council in this proposed draft. Yet the fact that this draft was not simply issued through normal channels, but was submitted to the bishops' conferences for comment, again indicated that collegiality was now more than simply a word. The enthusiastic applause given Cardinals König and Döpfner for their profound theological critique of this text and their positive development of this problem indicated that the spirit of the Council was still alive and unchanged. Nonetheless, an unmistakable fatigue could be noticed. This could not be remedied even by such pleasant diversions as the performance of the Regensburg Cathedral Choir and the Vienna Choir boys. It was felt with more and more urgency that the period of planting had ended and the time for assimilation would now have to begin.

On December 7 the last four texts were passed: the *Pastoral Constitution on the Church in the Modern World*, the *Decree on the Ministry and Life of Priests*, the *Decree on the Church's Missionary Activity*, and the *Declaration on*

Religious Liberty. There was an obvious spirit of joyous gratitude on the part of the bishops as they met for the last time in St. Peter's Basilica. There was an almost effusive atmosphere of joy when at the end they all embraced and gave one another the kiss of peace before departing. That morning, quite apart from the almost unexpected harvest of the four last highly controversial texts, the Council had again experienced one of its greatest hours, in which the breath of history was felt as rarely ever before. The Pope and the Patriarch of Constantinople had agreed "to regret and remove both from memory and the midst of the Church" the event which initiated the fateful split between East and West. This was the ban which had been imposed on July 16, 1054, by the papal legates on the Patriarch of Constantinople and the ban imposed by him on the legates. Amid the profound silence of the listening Council fathers and the many guests of this moving hour, Cardinal Bea read a joint declaration which was simultaneously read by the first secretary of the Holy Synod in Constantinople:

Since they are certain that they express the common desire for justice and the unanimous sentiment of charity which moves the faithful, and since they recall the command of the Lord: "If you are offering your gift at the altar, and there remember that your brother has something against you, leave your gift before the altar, and go, first be reconciled to your brother" (Mt. 5, 23-24), Pope Paul VI and Patriarch Athenagoras I with his Synod, in common agreement, declare that:

> (a) They regret the offensive words, the reproaches without foundation, and the reprehensible gestures which, on both sides, have marked or accompanied the sad events of this period.
>
> (b) They likewise regret and remove both from memory and from the midst of the Church the sentences of excommunication which followed these events, the memory of which has influenced actions up to our day and has hindered closer relations in charity, and they commit these excommunications to oblivion.
>
> (c) Finally, they deplore the preceding and later vexing events which, under the influence of various factors—among which were lack of understanding and mutual trust—eventually led to the effective rupture of ecclesiastical communion....

The tumultuous applause which greeted the symbolic kiss between the Pope and Metropolitan Meliton of Heliopolis, the representative of Patriarch Athenagoras, was mitigated only by the emotion that overwhelmed perhaps every participant of this historic moment. This

THEOLOGICAL HIGHLIGHTS OF VATICAN II

common burying of past guilt in forgiveness and forget-fulness, expressed in a brotherly embrace, stands as a sign of hope at the end of the Council. The millennium of hostility was spanned by the rainbow of reconciliation; the kiss of peace concluded the millennium which began with the curse of anathema.

Compared with the greatness of the final Council ocssion proper, the celebration of December 8, the closing day, which took place under the mild sun of Rome in St. Peter's Square, appeared somewhat pompous. The jubilee indulgences proclaimed for the months following the Council can be accepted as the exultant and baroque final cord of the whole affair. The real post-conciliar task though goes much deeper. What happened in Rome was only the formulation of a mandate whose execution must now be undertaken.

VI
—

EPILOGUE

Drawing up a balance sheet for the Council would require a book of its own. It would also be a little premature of us to attempt this. The analysis would have to include the unwritten as well as the written results of the Council. The results would have to be compared with the expectations and hopes of the Council as well as with the actual aims and aspirations and possibilities of both the Council and the Church in our time. Such an analysis would have to consider above all that the Council essentially sought only to set up a new framework, while practical implementation was left to the "directorates" (post-conciliar commissions) and to the bishops' conferences. This is the reason why, though the concrete results of the Council may appear so far rather meager, the overall result can be summed up in line with what Oscar Cullmann, the Protestant exegete from Basel, said to the German Council conference on December 2, 1965. After a careful analysis he said that, looking at the Council in retrospect, "on the whole our expectations, insofar as they were not based on illusions and apart from some exceptions, were fulfilled and in some respects surpassed."

A brief comment on the present situation of the Church and the Christian people in it may conclude these reflections. Wherever the Council is positively valued and its initiative joyously seized upon, almost always a certain unwitting injustice creeps in. I do not refer to the fact that here and there (and perhaps not so rarely) renewal is mistakenly taken to mean dilution and cheapening of religion. I do not mean that here and there we find overzealousness in reform of the liturgy which brings with it an evasion of the deeper demands of divine worship and thus makes light of and discredits the great vocation to genuine reform. I do not mean that here and there people seem to demand not so much truth as modernity, and they take this as the sufficient standard for behavior. These are all real dangers which, as Cullmann rightly suggested in the press conference mentioned above, should not be left to the integrists and the enemies of renewal to fight against. What I do have in mind is something much less conspicuous, I think—the tendency to picture everything in black and white. A positive summation of the Council almost inevitably leads to this, by emphasizing the Council's progress and contrasting the new gains made with the much less satisfactory state of affairs prior to the Council. Even now we sometimes hear the faithful complain that they are fed up with hearing sermons which follow the stereotyped pattern: "Of old it was said to you....But I say to you...."

I think it important that, with all our satisfaction over the Council's work of renewal, we not overlook certain ingredients of injustice, those little touches of Pharisaism which all too readily accompany this joy. Very much indeed did the Church need renewal from within in the new situation of today. Yet it must not be forgotten that the Church has always remained the Church, and that at any time in history the way of the gospel could be found and was found in it. I might make here an entirely personal remark to illustrate this point. In the fall of 1959 I remember reading in Friedrich Heiler's *Compendium of World Religions* an evaluation of the Catholic Church written by the editor, himself a former Catholic. He pointed out that, despite all the burdens of the past and despite all the dubiousness of the dogmas and methods of the Church (as Heiler saw it), yet it must be said that "many millions of people considered the Roman Church their spiritual mother, in whose bosom they feel protected in life as well as death." These words affected me very deeply at the time because I had shortly before witnessed a Christian death which revealed how true this is. This is great and wonderful—this protection that the Church is able to offer in life and in death. It seems to me of first importance, especially in the time after the Council, never to forget this fact. In the final analysis the Church lives, in sad as well as joyous times, from the faith of those who are simple of heart. This is the way that Israel lived even in the times when Pharisaic legalism and Sadducean liberalism defaced the countenance of the chosen people. Faith remained alive in those who were simple of heart. It was they who passed the torch of hope on to the New Testament. Their names are at once the last names of the old People of God and the first names of the new People—Zechariah, Elizabeth, Joseph and Mary. The faith of those who are simple of heart is the most precious treasure of the Church. To serve and to live this faith is the noblest vocation in the renewal of the Church.

Notes to Part Four

1. The close of section 3 of this note states that the pope "proceeds according to his own discretion and in view of the Church's welfare in structuring, promoting and endorsing the exercise of collegiality." Section 4 begins with the statement that the pope as supreme pastor can "always exercise his authority as he sees fit" and "as required by his office" (cf. W. Abbott, ed., *The Documents of Vatican II*: New York: America Press, 1966). Comparing this to the *motu proprio Apostolica sollicitudo*, which established the bishops' synod, we find a clear connection between the closing statement of section 3 of the "explanatory note" and part 3.1 of the *motu proprio*: the *motu proprio* sees the establishing of the synod as "structuring, promoting and endorsing the exercise of collegiality." Thus it seems that the collegial idea is indirectly introduced into the *motu proprio*—and in a place where we would least expect to find it.

2. This program was never wholly accepted. The Council—very fortunately—avoided any such complete systematizing of its teaching; it let the individual texts stand independently of one another. It thus averted the danger of a narrow ecclesiastical focus and

of mere self-analysis by the Church. It was primarily through the *Constitution on Divine Revelation* that the whole Council and its teaching on the Church were opened up to the teaching of God, before whom even the Church itself is only a listener. "Hearing the Word of God with reverence," the text begins, and thus in the final analysis all the Council's teaching is epitomized in a gesture of listening.

3. Section 36: "For by the very circumstance of their having been created, all things are endowed with their own stability, truth, goodness, proper laws and order. Man must respect these as he isolates them by the appropriate methods of the individual sciences or arts....Consequently, we cannot but deplore certain habits of mind, sometimes also found among Christians, which do not sufficiently attend to the rightful independence of science. The arguments and controversies which they spark lead many minds to conclude that faith and science are mutually opposed." Cf. section 42: "Christ, to be sure, gave his Church no proper mission in the political, economic or social order. The purpose which he set before it is a religious one." In section 76 we find application to the political sphere: "The role and competence of the Church being what it is, it must in no way be confused with the political community or bound to any political system. For it is at once a sign and a safeguard of the transcendence of the human person. In their proper spheres, the political community and the Church are mutually

THEOLOGICAL HIGHLIGHTS OF VATICAN II

independent and autonomous" (cf. W. Abbott, *op. cit.,* pp. 233-34, 241, 287-88).

4. African bishops especially pointed out this danger in their conversations after the Council discussion. In fact we would have to say that the personalistic stress in the contemporary theology of marriage may sometimes risk overlooking the essentially social significance of marriage. Thus the personalists can easily slide into their own kind of artificial construction— foreign both to reality and to revelation.

5. Section 80, 4th paragraph: "Any act of war aimed indiscriminately at the destruction of entire cities or of extensive areas and their population is a crime against God and against man himself. It deserves unequivocal and unhesitating condemnation" (cf. W. Abbott, *op. cit.,* p. 294). Pius XII said virtually the same thing in an address given on September 30, 1954 (*AAS* 46 [1954], p. 589). Further documentation can be found in footnote 2 of the Constitution. Cardinal Spellman, together with nine other fathers, objected in a note to the "pacifist tendencies" of sections 80-81 of the text. They asked for the rejection of the entire chapter on war and peace, and if necessary of the entire schema. A counter-presentation was offered by Archbishop Garonne, who was in charge of the overall editing of the schema, and Bishop Schröffer, head of the responsible subcommission. They rejected the charges as unfounded. Despite this the chapter received 483 *no* votes when it was specifically voted on (as against 1,710 *yes* votes and 8 invalid

ballots). But the eventual success of the schema was not obstructed by this action.

6. Especially misleading here was the formula suggested by H. R. Schlette to the effect that while the other religions are the ordinary way to salvation, the Church is the extraordinary way (*Die Religionen als Thema der Theologie* [Freiburg, 1964], p. 85). In the context of Schlette's balanced treatment this formula loses much of its offensive character. For the reaction against the tendency toward "optimism," cf., for example, H. Van Straelen, *Our Attitude Towards Other Religions* (Tokyo, 1965), pp. 79-115.